The Last Things

The Last Things

AN ESCHATOLOGY FOR LAYMEN

by

George Eldon Ladd

William B. Eerdmans Publishing Company

LIBRARY OF CONGRESS CATALOGING IN PUBLICATION DATA

Ladd, George Eldon, 1911-
  The last things.

  1. Eschatology. I. Title.
BT821.2.L32   236   77-15547
ISBN 0-8028-1727-0

CONTENTS

5

I

HOW TO INTERPRET THE PROPHETIC SCRIPTURES

BEFORE WE CAN ENTER INTO A STUDY OF WHAT THE BIBLE teaches about the last things, we are faced with the question of methodology. How shall we construct our eschatology? Evangelicals recognize that the Bible is inspired by the Holy Spirit and constitutes our only infallible rule for faith and practice. But what does this mean when we ask what the Bible teaches about various doctrinal themes, especially about eschatology?

Many evangelicals feel that the inspiration of the *whole* Bible leads to the conclusion that the whole Bible is of equal theological value. The many prophecies of the Bible are like the pieces of a jig-saw puzzle which only need to be fitted together to give us a grand mosaic of God's redemptive purposes both for the present and for the future.

A bit of reflection shows, however, that this procedure is impossible. The two Testaments have very different themes for their subject matter. The Old Testament is primarily concerned with the people of Israel — the elect descendants of Abraham — whom God called to be his peculiar people. Israel constituted a nation among other nations with a monarchy, a temple, and a priesthood. The Old Testament is primarily the story of this nation, her wars with other nations, her religious revivals and apostasies, her final political defeat and captivity at the hands of Assyria and Babylon, and finally the return of a remnant of the people to their land in Palestine in the days of Ezra and Nehemiah.

Throughout the period of the monarchy and captivity prophets appeared among the people of Israel to proclaim God's judgment upon the nation because of her apostasy, but also to announce that Israel's apostasy was not final and irremedial. In the indeterminate future God would bring about a revival among the people so that they would turn in repentance and obedience to him. This would in turn result in God's favor upon the nation, and Israel would be restored in peace and prosperity to inherit the land. In the Old Testament the eschatological salvation is always pictured in terms of the national, theocratic fate of the people Israel. *There are no clear prophecies of the Christian church as such in the Old Testament.* The Gentiles do indeed have a place in Israel's future, but there is no uniform concept in the Old Testament of what that place will be. Sometimes the Gentiles will be subdued by force and compelled to serve Israel (Amos 9:12; Mic. 5:9-13; 7:16-17; Isa. 45:14-16; 49:23; 60:12,14). On other occasions the Gentiles are seen as being converted to the faith of Israel so as to serve Israel's God (Zeph. 3:9, 20; Isa. 2:2-4; 42:6-7; 60:1-14; Zech. 8:20-23; 14:16-19). Israel remains the people of God, and the future salvation is first of all Israel's salvation.

When we turn to the New Testament, we meet a very different situation. Jesus offered himself to Israel as her Messiah only to be rejected and finally crucified. As a result, "the kingdom of God will be taken away from you [Israel] and given to a nation producing the fruits of it" (Matt. 21:43). However, a remnant of the people did respond to his message and became his disciples. Acts tells the story of the birthday of the church at Pentecost; but this church was radically different from Israel. Instead of being a nation, the church was an open fellowship of people who believed that Jesus was the Messiah. At first the church consisted largely of Jews, but Acts tells the

8

story of how the church moved out into the Gentile world, accepted many Gentiles into its fellowship, and concludes with the story of Paul preaching to a largely Gentile church in Rome. Eschatology in the New Testament deals largely with the destiny of the church.

Here we have two different stories: the story of the nation Israel and the story of the church. What are we to make of this apparent dilemma?

Two radically different answers have been proposed, and every student of prophecy must choose between them. The first is to conclude that God has two different programs: one for Israel and one for the church. Israel was and remains and is to be a theocratic people who are destined to inherit the promised land of Palestine, for whom Jesus will be the literal Davidic king, when the prophecies of the Old Testament will be literally fulfilled. This system is called *Dispensationalism.* It is commonly thought that the main tenet of Dispensationalism is a series of dispensations or time periods in which God deals in different ways with his people. This, however, is incorrect. Judged by this norm, every Bible student must be a Dispensationalist. There are the eras of promise after Abraham, of law under Moses, of grace under Christ, and of the Kingdom of God in the future. Rather, the two chief tenets of Dispensationalism are that there are two peoples of God for whom God has two different programs and destinies — theocratic and earthly for Israel, spiritual and heavenly for the church. (See C. C. Ryrie, *Dispensationalism Today,* Moody, 1965, p. 97.)

The second way of interpreting prophecy is to recognize progressive revelation and to interpret the Old Testament by the New Testament. Dispensationalists usually refer to this as covenantal theology because it emphasizes the element of unity between the Old and the New Covenants. However, the present writer who supports this method does not do so because he was raised in covenantal theology; in fact, in his earliest years he was a Dispensationalist. It has been through his own inductive study of the Bible that he has become convinced that the Old Testament must be interpreted (and often reinterpreted) by the new revelation given in the person and mission of Jesus Christ.

Before we apply this principle to eschatology, we will try to establish its validity by a survey of biblical Christology — its teaching about the Messiah.

There are three messianic personages in the Old Testament which stand side by side with no indication of how they relate to each other. The first is that of the Davidic King — in New Testament times called "the Messiah," "the Christ," "the Anointed One." This royal heir to the throne of David is vividly pictured in Isaiah 11. Isaiah sees a day when the family tree of the royal lineage of Jesse, the father of David, would be fallen. It would look as if the messianic hopes of David's heirs were frustrated. But out of the stump of the fallen tree would spring forth a new shoot, a new branch, a new kingly heir. "The Spirit of the Lord shall rest upon him," bestowing upon him wisdom, understanding, and knowledge. This would in turn enable him to rule over his people with true justice, righteousness, and equity. His primary mission would be that of a just king. Not only would he rule over his people righteously; he would be so endowed as to destroy the enemies of God and God's people. "He shall smite the earth with the rod of his mouth, and with the breath of his lips he shall slay the wicked." The result will be a rule of peace and blessedness. The curse will be removed from nature. Fierce beasts will lose their ferocity. "The wolf shall dwell with the lamb, and the leopard shall lie down with the kid, and the calf and the lion and the fatling together, and a little child shall lead them." This, however, is only one aspect of his kingdom. "The earth shall be full of the knowledge of the Lord as the waters cover the sea." This will in turn mean the salvation of the Gentiles. "In that day the root of Jesse shall stand as an ensign to the peoples; him shall the nations seek, and his dwelling shall be glorious."

10

There is no word here of a humble prophet of Nazareth who went about as a man among men, teaching, healing, helping. There is no word here of an eternal, preexistent divine being who became flesh and dwelt among us. There is no word here of a humble servant who suffered death for the sins of man. The entire emphasis is upon his victorious rule — his vanquishing of wicked men, his establishing peace and righteousness in all the earth.

This certainly is the obvious meaning of the passage, and it is how the Jews of Jesus' day understood it. In the years of the Maccabees and their successors (163-64 B.C.), the Jews achieved independence from their Syrian masters (the Seleucids) and became once again a powerful independent nation with kings reigning over them. But in 63 B.C. Rome extended her iron hand into Palestine in the person of Pompey, captured Jerusalem, slew many of the Jewish people, and sent many others back as prisoners of war to Rome. At this time, an unknown Jewish writer penned these words:

> Behold, O Lord, and raise up unto them their king, the son of David,
> At the time in which Thou seest, O God, that he may reign over Israel, Thy servant.
> And gird him with strength, that he may shatter unrighteous rulers,
> And that he may purge Jerusalem from nations that trample her down to destruction.
> Wisely and righteously he shall thrust out sinners from the inheritance.
> He shall destroy the pride of the sinner as a potter's vessel,
> With a rod of iron he shall break in pieces all their substance.
> He shall destroy the godless nations with the word of his mouth;
> At his rebuke nations shall flee before him,
> And he shall reprove sinners for the thoughts of their hearts....
> And there shall be no unrighteousness in his days in their midst,

11

For all shall be holy and their king the anointed of the Lord.

(Ps. Solomon 17:23 ff.)

The poet is expressing the prevailing expectation of the Lord's Anointed, the Lord's Christ in New Testament times. His chief role is to deliver God's people Israel from the hated yoke of the heathen nations.

This enables us to understand the perplexity of John the Baptist when he was imprisoned by Herod Antipas, who reigned in Galilee in the name of Rome. "Now when John heard in prison about the deeds of the Christ [the Messiah], he sent word by his disciples and said to him, 'Are you he who is to come, or shall we look for another?'" (Matt. 11:2-3). The deeds of the Messiah — what were they? Teaching, healing the sick, cleansing lepers, antagonizing the religious leaders of his day. But this was not what the Messiah was to do. He was to challenge hostile nations; he was to slay the wicked. How could he be Messiah when Herod Antipas was living in open adultery with his brother's wife? John had challenged him, and as a result was sent to prison and finally lost his life. Jesus did not challenge him. He did not challenge the Roman rule embodied in Judaea in the governor, Pontius Pilate. How then could Jesus be Messiah? He was doing many good works but none of the deeds expected of the Davidic Messiah. John did not lose his courage; John did not question God's call of him to proclaim the Coming One. Had not John himself announced, "The chaff he will burn with unquenchable fire" (Matt. 3:12)? John only questioned how Jesus could be the Messiah, for his deeds were not those of the expected King. Jesus, in fact, embodied a new revelation of God's purpose. He was indeed the Messiah, the Davidic King, but his mission was a spiritual mission — to deliver men from bondage to sin — rather than a political one — to deliver Israel from Rome.

A very different messianic picture is painted in the Christology of Daniel 7. In a vision, Daniel sees four beasts arising from the sea. These represent four successive world empires. Then Daniel sees in his vision the heavenly throne with God seated upon it. Then the world empires were destroyed. "I saw in the night visions, and behold, with the clouds of heaven there came one like a son of man, and he came to the Ancient of Days and was presented before him. And to him was given dominion and glory and kingdom, that all peoples, nations, and languages should serve him; his dominion is an everlasting dominion, which shall not pass away, and his kingdom one that shall not be destroyed" (Dan. 7:13-14).

Whether this figure "like a son of man" is an individual or, like the four beasts, a symbol representing the people of God is not important for our discussion. Whichever it is, we know from contemporary sources that certain circles in Judaism interpreted this figure in individualistic terms. The Son of Man becomes a heavenly, preexistent, supernatural figure who has been preserved in the presence of God. In God's time, he will come to earth to raise the dead, to judge the wicked, to redeem God's people and gather them into a glorious, everlasting kingdom.

The first thing to be emphasized is that this is a very different concept from that of the Davidic Messiah. To be sure, twice in our sources the Son of Man is called the Messiah, but this represented a tendency obvious in Judaism to conflate diverse messianic concepts. The Messiah is a son of David; the Son of Man is a supernatural being. The Messiah is a son of David; the Son of Man is a supernatural being. The Messiah arises as a man among men; the Son of Man comes from heaven. The Messiah rules in an earthy kingdom of peace and righteousness; the Son of Man raises the dead and rules in a glorious kingdom on a transformed earth. These two figures are utterly diverse, and, on the surface at least, mutually exclusive.

Against this background we can understand the confusion of the disciples when Jesus began to use the term "the Son of Man" to designate his own mission and ministry. When Jesus pronounced the sins of a paralytic man forgiven, the Jews thought he was guilty of blasphemy.

13

"Who can forgive sins but God alone?" (Mark 2:7). In reply, Jesus said, " 'But that you may know that the Son of man has authority on earth to forgive sins' — he said to the paralytic — 'I say to you, rise, take up your pallet and go home' " (Mark 2:10-11). Again, when he and his disciples were criticized for picking grain on the sabbath, he said, "The sabbath was made for man and not man for the sabbath; so the Son of man is lord even of the sabbath" (Mark 2:27-28).

Such language was utterly confusing. How could Jesus be the Son of Man? The Son of Man was a preexistent heavenly being who would reign in a glorious kingdom. Everybody knew who Jesus was — the son of a carpenter from Nazareth. What did he have in common with the Son of Man?

Later Jesus uttered a number of sayings that were more like Daniel's prophecy. "For whoever is ashamed of me and of my words in this adulterous and sinful generation, of him will the Son of man also be ashamed when he comes in the glory of his Father with the holy angels" (Mark 8:38). "And then they will see the Son of man coming in clouds with great power and glory. And then he will send out the angels, and gather his elect from the four winds, from the ends of the earth to the ends of heaven" (Mark 13:26-27).

This language made sense to the disciples. A heavenly figure, coming in clouds with power and great glory to gather God's people into the Kingdom of God — this they understood. But what did such a heavenly figure have to do with Jesus? The Son of Man was a preexistent figure in the presence of God. Jesus was the son of the carpenter of Nazareth. What did he have in common with the Son of Man? And what could either one have in common with the Davidic King?

But this is not all. There is a third personage in the Old Testament who carries messianic dimensions — the Suffering Servant. He is pictured in Isaiah 53. He was humble and passive. "He was oppressed, and he was afflicted, yet

14

he opened not his mouth; like a lamb that is led to the slaughter, like a sheep that before its shearers is dumb, so he opened not his mouth." He was oppressed and marred by suffering. "He had no form or comeliness that we should look at him, and no beauty that we should desire him. He was despised and rejected by men; a man of sorrows and acquainted with grief." He was to meet an untimely death. "He was cut off from the land of the living, stricken for the transgressions of my people, and they made his grave with the wicked." However, his sufferings were undeserved, vicarious. He suffered for the sins of his people. "But he was wounded for our transgressions, he was bruised for our iniquities; upon him was the chastisement that made us whole, and with his stripes we are healed." "The Lord has laid on him the iniquity of us all." "He was stricken for the transgressions of my people." "He makes himself an offering for sin." He shall "make many to be accounted righteous; and he shall bear their iniquities." "He bore the sin of many, and made intercession for the transgressors."

The first thing to be noted about this great chapter is that the suffering one is not identified with the Messiah. He is not called an anointed one; there is no reference to the family tree of David. In fact, in the prelude to the chapter (52:13), he is simply called God's servant. "Behold, my servant shall prosper, he shall be exalted and lifted up, and shall be very high." In the context in which this chapter is found, the servant is often identified as Israel. "You are my servant, Israel, in whom I will be glorified" (Isa. 49:3). "The Lord has redeemed his servant Jacob!" (Isa. 48:20). "For the sake of my servant Jacob, and Israel my chosen, I call you by your name" (Isa. 45:4). Again, the servant is one who redeems unfaithful Israel. "And now the Lord says, who formed me from the womb to be his servant, that Israel might be gathered to him" (Isa. 49:5; see also 49:6). It seems that the servant concept fluctuates between the corporate concept, Israel, and the individual who redeems Israel.

However, the fact remains: the Suffering Servant of Isaiah 53 seems clearly to be someone other than the Davidic messianic King and the heavenly Son of Man. How can Messiah at one and the same time be one who smites the earth with the rod of his mouth and slays the wicked with the breath of his lips, and also be one who is smitten, who helplessly and passively suffers death? It was only the mission of Jesus which conflated the three Old Testament messianic ideas.

Little wonder that the disciples were slow to grasp the messiahship of Jesus. This is the significance of Peter's confession at Caesarea Philippi when he as spokesman for all the disciples recognized the messiahship of Jesus. Peter means to say that in spite of the fact that Jesus was not acting like a conquering Davidic King, he was nevertheless the Messiah in whom the Old Testament hope was being fulfilled. After the miracle of the feeding of the five thousand with a few loaves and fishes, there arose a popular movement to take Jesus by force and make him king (John 6:15). Here indeed was a man divinely endowed. Give him a few swords and spears and he could multiply them and equip an army. Pilate's troops would be unable to stand before him. However, this was not Jesus' present mission. *As the Son of Man, he had come to be the Suffering Servant, and only after this mission of suffering to be the heavenly Son of Man.* Jesus began to instruct his disciples in this fact immediately after Caesarea Philippi. He was indeed the Messiah, the Davidic King, but it was not his mission at present to rule from the throne of David. "He was teaching his disciples, saying to them, 'The Son of man will be delivered into the hands of men, and they will kill him' " (Mark 9:31). "For the Son of man came not to be served but to serve, and to give his life as a ransom for many" (Mark 10:45). Here was a message the disciples were not prepared for. There is no evidence that Jews in Jesus' day interpreted Isaiah 53 messianically. Indeed, the two concepts seem to be mutually exclusive. How could a heavenly, supernatural Son of Man, destined to rule in God's glorious kingdom, be a humble, submissive man, taunted and tortured and finally put to death by his enemies? It seemed impossible.

But precisely here is our basic hermeneutic. Jesus, and the apostles after him, reinterpreted the Old Testament prophecies in light of Jesus' person and mission. *The Son of Man must appear on earth before he comes in glory, and his earthly mission was to fill the role of the Suffering Servant.*

This reinterpretation is not confined to Jesus' teaching; it was furthered by the apostles in an equally unforeseen way. After Jesus' death the disciples experienced his resurrection and ascension and then Pentecost. On the day of Pentecost Peter preached an amazing sermon. He reinterpreted passages from Psalm 16:8-11 and Psalm 132:11 which in their Old Testament context speak of David's hope that death would not be the end of existence.

> "Being therefore a prophet, and knowing that God had sworn with an oath to him that he would set one of his descendants upon his throne, he foresaw and spoke of the resurrection of the Christmas. . . . Being therefore exalted at the right hand of God, and having received from the Father the promise of the Holy Spirit, he has poured out this which you see and hear. For David did not ascend into the heavens; but he himself says, 'The Lord said to my Lord, Sit at my right hand till I make thy enemies a stool for thy feet.' Let all the house of Israel therefore know assuredly that God has made him both Lord and Christ, this Jesus whom you crucified." (Acts 2:30-36)

Here is an amazing bit of reinterpretation of Old Testament prophecy. The promise in Psalm 110:1-2, "The Lord says to my lord: 'Sit at my right hand, till I make your enemies your footstool'" refers to the king's throne in Jerusalem, as the next verse proves: "The Lord sends forth from Zion your mighty scepter. Rule in the midst of your foes" (Ps. 110:2). Peter, under inspiration, transfers the throne of David from its earthly site in Jerusalem to heaven itself. This verse became a favorite verse used by the author of Hebrews to affirm the triumphal session of Jesus at the right hand of God in heaven (Heb. 1:13, 10:12,13). Peter's summary affirmation, "God has made him both Lord and Christ" (Acts 2:36) asserts the same truth. "Lord" means absolute sovereign. "Christ" means Messiah or Davidic King. By his resurrection and ascension, Jesus has entered into his messianic reign. "For he must reign [as King] until he has put all his enemies under his feet" (I Cor. 15:25). "He who conquers, I will grant him to sit with me on my throne, as I myself conquered and sat down with my Father on his throne" (Rev. 3:21). That Lord and King are basically interchangeable terms is proven by Revelation 17:14 where it is said of the conquering Lamb, "for he is Lord of lords and King of kings." By his resurrection and ascension, Jesus has entered into a new experience of his messiahship. On earth, he had been the meek, humble Suffering Servant. Now he is enthroned at God's right hand. Now that his messianic sufferings are past, he has entered in upon his messianic reign, and he will continue that reign until all enemies have been subdued (I Cor. 15:25). The character of this messianic reign was unforeseen in the Old Testament. There his reign is from Jerusalem, over Israel. "The Lord swore to David a sure oath from which he will not turn back: 'One of the sons of your body I will set on your throne'" (Ps. 132:11). In the New Testament his reign is from heaven and is universal in its scope.

We trust that this excursion into Christology has proved the point we wish to make, namely, that the Old Testament prophets must be interpreted in light of their fulfillment in the person and mission of Jesus. We have seen that this involves *re*interpretation. Sometimes the fulfillment is different from what we would expect from the Old Testament.

In other words, the final word in doctrine, whether in Christology or eschatology, must be found in the New Testament.

II

WHAT ABOUT ISRAEL?

IN THE FIRST CHAPTER WE ESTABLISHED THE PRINCIPLE OF biblical hermeneutics: the Old Testament must be interpreted in light of the new revelation given in Jesus Christ. What then does the New Testament teach about Israel? If the Old Testament sees the future salvation of Israel, does the New Testament reinterpret these prophecies so radically that they are to be fulfilled spiritually in the church? Is the church the new and true Israel? Or does God still have a future for his people Israel?

We are fortunate to have in the inspired Scripture a lengthy discussion of this theme in Romans 9-11. Paul first expresses his heart-felt concern and love for his kinsmen after the flesh. He says, "I have great sorrow and unceasing anguish in my heart" (Rom. 9:2) for Israel because they have rejected Jesus as their Messiah.

His first point is that "Israel," that is, the true spiritual Israel—the people of God—is not identical with the physical offspring of Abraham. "For not all who are descended from Israel [natural seed] belong to Israel [spiritual seed], and not all are children of Abraham because they are his descendants" (Rom. 9:6-7). Paul recalls Old Testament history to prove this. Abraham had two sons, Isaac and Esau. However, even though the family of Esau and his descendants are the natural seed of Abraham, they are not included in the spiritual seed; but "through Isaac shall your descendants be named" (Rom. 9:7). "This means that it is not the children of the flesh who are the children of God but the children of promise are reckoned as descendants" (Rom. 9:8). God chose Isaac but rejected Esau. Therefore the true descendants of Abraham — the true Israel — must be determined not by natural physical descent, but by the divine election and promise of God.

The implication is clear. Not all Jews of Paul's day can call themselves "Israel," the people of God, but only those who emulate Abraham's faith, and so prove themselves to be children of promise.

This principle has already been enunciated earlier in the Roman epistle. In Romans 2:28-29, Paul writes, "For he is not a real Jew who is one outwardly, nor is true circumcision something external and physical. He is a Jew who is one inwardly, and real circumcision is a matter of the heart, spiritual and not literal."

This principle of spiritual *vs.* physical circumcision is not original with Paul. He is repeating a theme already found in the Old Testament: "Circumcise yourselves to the Lord, remove the foreskin of your hearts, O men of Judah and inhabitants of Jerusalem, lest my wrath go forth like fire, and burn with none to quench it, because of the evil of your doings" (Jer. 4:4). External obedience to the law of Moses does not make one a member of the true sons of Abraham, assuring him of the favor of God; there must be a heart — and a life — to match. Otherwise he will face the wrath of God.

This principle is applied in two verses in the Revelation of John. John speaks of "those who say they are Jews and are not, but are a synagogue of Satan" (Rev. 2:9; cf. also 3:9). Here are people who (rightly) claim to be Jews. While they are physically and religiously Jews, John says that they are not spiritually Jews but are in fact a synagogue of Satan, because they reject Jesus as their Messiah and persecute his disciples.

Paul next meets the objection that if this is true, it reflects an arbitrary action on the part of God. Paul answers in strong language. God is God, the creator of men, and as such has a right to do as he pleases with his creatures. "But, who are you, a man, to answer back to God? Will what is molded say to its molder, 'Why have you made me thus?' Has the potter no right over the clay, to make out of the same lump one vessel for beauty and another for menial use?" (Rom. 9:20-21). This verse is often interpreted in terms of God's election and rejection to the salvation of the individual. However, whatever may be the application to the individual, Paul's thought is primarily about redemptive history and God's election of Jacob to be the heir of the promises given to Abraham. God has endured with much patience the rebellion and apostasy of literal Israel, "in order to make known the riches of his glory for the vessels of mercy, which he has prepared beforehand to glory" (Rom. 9:23). That is to say, God has been patient with the unbelief of literal Israel that through it he might show mercy upon true Israel. Paul picks up this idea later in the section. "So I ask, have they stumbled so as to fall [finally and irretrievably]? By no means. But through their trespass salvation has come to the Gentiles" (Rom. 11:11). God has a purpose in Israel's stumbling and unbelief. It was not that God had grown impatient and the fall of Israel occurred for its own sake. Rather, God used the fall of Israel to bring salvation to the Gentiles.

Paul carries this out in the earlier passage: "The vessels of mercy, which he has prepared for glory" consist not of the Jews only but also of Gentiles (Rom. 9:24). The "vessels of mercy" which God has chosen to take the place of the vessels of wrath — unbelieving Jews who stand under God's judgment — are a mixed company consisting of both Jews and Gentiles. Then Paul does an amazing thing. He quotes two passages from Hosea which in their Old Testament context refer to Israel and applies them to the Christian church which consists largely of Gentiles. And he does this to prove that the Old Testament foresees the Gentile church. "As indeed he says in Hosea, 'Those who were not my people I will call my people,

21

and her who was not beloved I will call my beloved' "
(Rom. 9:25).

Hosea had been commanded by the Lord to take a wife who was a harlot to symbolize Israel's spiritual harlotry. His second child was a girl, and Hosea was told, "Call her name Not pitied, for I will no more have pity on the house of Israel to forgive them at all" (Hos. 1:6).

However, this rejection of Israel is not final and irremediable. In fact, Hosea goes on to affirm the future salvation of Israel in the Kingdom of God. Hosea sees a day when violence will be removed from the animal kingdom. God will make a covenant with the beasts of the field, with the birds, and with creeping things. He will abolish the instruments of violence and warfare, the bow and the sword, indeed, war itself. Israel will dwell safely in the land; she will lie down in safety. "And I will betroth you to me forever; I will betroth you to me in righteousness and in justice, in steadfast love, and in mercy" (Hos. 2:19). Then Hosea says, "And I will have pity on Not pitied, and I will say to Not my people, 'You are my people'; and he shall say, 'Thou art my God' " (Hos. 2:23).

Here we have the same phenomenon in the area of eschatology which we found in Christology: Old Testament concepts are radically reinterpreted and given an unforeseen application. What in the Old Testament applies to literal Israel, in Romans 9:25 applies to the church, which consists not only of Jews but also of Gentiles (Rom. 9:24). In fact, the predominate structure of the New Testament church is Gentile.

Paul again quotes from Hosea: "And in the very place where it was said to them, 'You are not my people,' they will be called 'sons of the living God' " (Rom. 9:26). Hosea had a third child, a son, and was told, "Call his name Not my people, for you are not my people and I am not your God" (Hos. 1:9).

In this case, Hosea goes on immediately to announce the future salvation of Israel. "Yet the number of the people of Israel shall be like the sand of the sea which can be neither measured nor numbered; and in the place where it was said to them: 'You are not my people,' it shall be said to them, 'Sons of the living God' " (Hos. 1:10).

Here, in two separate places, prophecies which in their Old Testament context refer to literal Israel are in the New Testament applied to the (Gentile) church. In other words, Paul sees the spiritual fulfillment of Hosea 1:10 and 2:23 in the church. It follows inescapably that the salvation of the Gentile church is the fulfillment of prophecies made to Israel. Such facts as this are what compel some Bible students, including the present writer, to speak of the church as the New Israel, the true Israel, the spiritual Israel.

This conclusion is supported in passages where Paul speaks of Christian believers as (spiritual) children of Abraham. "The purpose was to make him [Abraham] the father of all who believe without being circumcised and who thus have righteousness reckoned to them, and likewise the father of the circumcised who are not merely circumcised but who follow the example of faith which our father Abraham had before he was circumcised" (Rom. 4:11-12). Here Abraham is said to be the father of believing Jews and believing Gentiles. The conclusion follows inescapably: it is believers, whether Jews or Greeks, who are the true children of Abraham — the true spiritual Israel. We are reminded again of Romans 2:28-29; real Jews are those who have been circumcised inwardly.

Again in Romans 4:16 Paul repeats, "For he [Abraham] is the father of us all." Writing to the Galatians, Paul had already stated this truth, "So you see that it is men of faith who are the sons of Abraham" (Gal. 3:7).

To Dispensationalists, a "spiritualizing" hermeneutic is the most dangerous way to interpret the Old Testament. Professor John Walvoord has written that this is the hermeneutic which characterizes modern Roman Catholic, modern liberal, and modern non-dispensational conservative writers (*The Millennial Kingdom,* Dunham, 1959, p.

71). The present writer feels that he must adopt a spiritualizing hermeneutic because he *finds the New Testament
applying to the spiritual church promises which in the
Old Testament refer to literal Israel*. He does not do this
because of any preconceived covenant theology but because he is bound by the Word of God.

If then the church is the true spiritual Israel, "has God
rejected his people" — literal Israel (Rom. 11:1)? Paul
goes on to answer this question at some length. He hints
at their future salvation in Romans 11:15, "For if their
rejection [of literal Israel] means reconciliation of the
world [salvation of the Gentiles], what will their accept-
ance mean but life from the dead?"

Paul goes on to illustrate this by the famous metaphor
of the olive tree. The olive tree is the people of God, seen
in its entirety. Natural branches (Jews) have been broken
off from their natural tree, and wild olive branches (Gentiles) have been grafted into the cultivated olive tree. But
whoever heard of grafting wild branches into a cultivated
tree? Paul is aware of this problem, for he says that it is
"contrary to nature" (Rom. 11:24). Paul warns the Gentiles who have taken the place of Israel not to boast over
Israel, for God is able to cut them off again. In the same
way, "even the others [Jews], if they do not persist in
their unbelief, will be grafted in, for God has the power
to graft them in again. For if you have been cut from
what is by nature a wild olive tree, and grafted, contrary
to nature, into a cultivated olive tree, how much more
will these natural branches be grafted back into their
own olive tree" (Rom. 11:23-24).

Then Paul summarizes the whole situation by a mag-
nificent statement: "Lest you be wise in your own con-
ceits, I want you to understand this mystery, brethren: a
hardening has come upon part of Israel, until the full
number of Gentiles come in, and so all Israel will be
saved; as it is written,

> *"The Deliverer will come from Zion,
> he will banish ungodliness from Jacob";*

24

WHAT ABOUT ISRAEL?

*"and this will be my covenant with them
when I take away their sins."* (Rom. 11:25-27)

Here is the divine order in redemptive history: natural branches on the cultivated olive tree; natural branches broken off because of unbelief; wild branches grafted in, contrary to nature; the natural branches yet to be re-grafted into the olive tree. Israel stumbled at the rock of offense — Christ — but not that she should forever fall (Rom. 11:11). When Paul says, "All Israel will be saved," he obviously cannot mean every Jew who ever lived. He is talking about redemptive history. But the day will come when "all Israel," the vast majority of living Jews, will be saved.

We could wish that Paul had written more about the way in which Israel will be saved. The words "the Deliverer will come from Zion" may well refer to the Second Coming of Christ. One of the purposes of his return will be to redeem Israel as well as to take the church unto himself.

However, two things are clear. *Israel must be saved in the same way as the church* — by turning in faith to Jesus as their Messiah (Rom. 11:23), and the blessings which Israel will experience are blessings *in Christ* — the same blessings which the church has experienced.

What then of the detailed promises in the Old Testament of a restored temple? The book of Hebrews clearly answers this question when it says that the law was "but a shadow of the good things to come instead of the true form of these realities . . ." (Heb. 10:1). The law with its temple and sacrificial system was only a shadow of the blessings — the reality — which has come to us in Christ. The shadow has fulfilled its purpose. Christ has now entered the true tabernacle in heaven where he presides as our great high priest. It is inconceivable that God's redemptive plan will revert to the age of shadows.

Indeed, Hebrews flatly affirms this. Here we read, "But as it is, Christ has obtained a ministry which is as much more excellent than the old as the covenant he mediates is better, since it is enacted on better promises. For if that first covenant had been faultless, there would have been no occasion for a second" (Heb. 8:6-7). The point to be emphasized is that Hebrews is contrasting the new covenant made in Christ with the Mosaic covenant. If the Mosaic covenant had been adequate, there would have been no need for a second covenant.

Hebrews proves this by a long quotation from Jeremiah 31:31-34.

> The days will come, says the Lord,
> when I will establish a new covenant with the house of
> Israel and with the house of Judah. . . .
> This is the covenant that I will make with the house of
> Israel after those days, says the Lord:
> I will put my laws into their minds,
> and write them on their hearts,
> and I will be their God,
> and they shall be my people. . . .
> For I will be merciful toward their iniquities,
> And I will remember their sins no more.

Here we have again the phenomenon we have already encountered. It is very difficult to believe there are two new covenants: the one made by Christ with the church through his shed blood, and a future new covenant to be made with Israel, which according to Dispensationalists is largely a renewal of the Mosaic covenant. To be sure, we have already found in Romans 9-11 that Paul teaches that literal Israel is yet to be brought within the new covenant; but it is the same new covenant made through the cross with the church. It is not a different covenant. Hebrews 8 applies a promise made through Jeremiah to the new covenant made by Christ with his church.

This is made doubly clear in a second passage. Hebrews 10:11-17 speaks of the sacrifice of Christ on the cross for sins, his subsequent session at the right hand of God, "then to wait until his enemies should be made a stool for his feet. For by a single offering he has perfected for all time those who are sanctified" (Heb. 10:13-14). These words make it indisputable that Hebrews is talking about the covenant made by Christ with his church. Then Hebrews quotes again from Jeremiah 31.

> "*This is the covenant that I will make with them*
> *after those days, says the Lord:*
> *I will put my laws on their hearts,*
> *and write them on their minds,"*
> *then he adds,*
> "*I will remember their sins and their misdeeds no more."*

Where there is forgiveness of these, there is no longer any offering for sin. (Heb. 10:16-18)

It is difficult to see how anyone can deny that the new covenant of Jeremiah 31 is the new covenant made by Christ with his church.

The passage we have just cited from Hebrews says that when there is forgiveness, there is no longer any offering for sin. The forgiveness wrought by Christ renders invalid and obsolete the Mosaic system. Hebrews asserts the same truth in 8:13: "In speaking of a new covenant, he treats the first as obsolete. And what is becoming obsolete and growing old is ready to vanish away." Whether or not these words refer to the historical destruction of Jerusalem by the Romans in 70 A.D., they at least affirm the dissolution of the old Mosaic order, because the new order of redemptive reality has come.

Here again we have a radical reinterpretation of the Old Testament prophets which speaks of the impermanence of the Mosaic covenant with its temple and sacrificial system. The argument of Hebrews is that these are types and shadows pointing to the spiritual reality which has come in Christ. Once the types and shadows have fulfilled their purpose, they are discarded in God's redemptive programs.

What does this have to do with the present Israeli question? Three things: First, God has preserved his people. Israel remains a "holy" people (Rom. 11:16), set apart and destined to carry out the divine purpose. Second, all Israel is yet to be saved. One modern scholar has suggested that in the millennium history may witness for the

27

first time a truly Christian nation. Third, the salvation of Israel must be through the new covenant made in the blood of Christ already established with the church, not through a rebuilt Jewish temple with a revival of the Mosaic sacrificial system. Hebrews flatly affirms that the whole Mosaic system is obsolete and about to pass away. Therefore the popular Dispensational position that Israel is the "clock of prophecy" is misguided. Possibly the modern return of Israel to Palestine is a part of God's purpose for Israel, but the New Testament sheds no light on this problem. However, the preservation of Israel as a people through the centuries is a sign that God has not cast off his people Israel.

III

THE INTERMEDIATE STATE

There's a land beyond the river
That they call the sweet forever,
And we only reach that shore by faith's decree;
One by one we reach the portals,
There to dwell with the immortals,
When they ring those golden bells for you and me.

THIS OLD EVANGELISTIC SONG EXPRESSES THE IDEA MANY Christians have of life after death. When we die, "we go to heaven." The popular idea is that heaven is a state of blessedness — "the sweet forever" — through whose portals the man of faith passes when he dies and crosses the river of death. There, in a state of disembodied blessedness, he will "dwell with the immortals."

Such thinking, popular as it is, is more an expression of Greek thought than of biblical theology. The Greeks — at least many of them who followed in the philosophical tradition of Plato — believed in a cosmic dualism. There were two worlds — the seen and the unseen, the visible and the invisible, the phenomenal and the noumenal. The visible world was a realm of ebb and flow, flux and change, instability, having only the appearance of reality. The unseen world was the world of permanence, of ultimate reality. In the same way man was a dualism of body and soul. The body belongs to the phenomenal world, the soul to the noumenal world. The body was not evil per se as in later Gnosticism but was a bur-

29

den and a hindrance to the soul. *Soma-sema:* the body was the tomb of the soul. The wise man was he who learned to discipline and subdue the passions and appetites of the body and cultivate the soul, the highest faculty of which was mind. "Salvation" — a biblical, not a Greek concept — meant that at death the soul would be liberated from the body and take its flight to the noumenal world.

The biblical idea of the world and man is very different. Fundamental to Old Testament thought is the belief that God is the creator, that the world is God's world and is therefore in itself good. "And God saw that it [creation] was good" (Gen. 1:12, 18, 21, 25, 31). The world was created for God's glory (Ps. 19:1); the ultimate goal and destiny of creation is to glorify and praise the creator (Ps. 98:7-9). The Hebrews had no concept of nature; to them the world was the scene of God's constant activity. Thunder was the voice of God (Ps. 29:3-5); pestilence was the heavy hand of the Lord (I Sam. 5:6); human breath is the breath of God inbreathed in man's face (Gen. 2:7; Ps. 104:29).

The Old Testament never views the earth as an alien place nor as an indifferent theater on which man lives out his temporal life while seeking a heavenly destiny. Man and the world together belong to the order of creation; in a real sense of the word, the world *participates* in man's fate. There is no antithesis between physical and spiritual life, between the inner and the outer dimensions in man, between the lower and higher realms. Life is viewed in its wholeness as the full enjoyment of all of God's gifts. Some Christian theologians would consider this crassly materialistic; but a profound theology underlies it. Life, which can be enjoyed only from the perspective of obedience to God and love for him (Deut. 30:1-3) means physical prosperity and productivity (Deut. 30:9); a long life (Ps. 34:12; 91:16); bodily health and well being (Prov. 4:22; 22:4); physical security (Deut. 8:1); in brief, the enjoyment of all of God's gifts (Ps. 103:1-5). However, the enjoyment of these good things by themselves cannot be called life, for life means the enjoyment of God's gifts *in fellowship with God*. It is God alone who is the source of all good things including life itself (Ps. 36:9). Those who forsake the Lord will be put to shame, for they have abandoned the fountain of life (Jer. 17:13). While health and bodily well-being are included in all that life means, man does not live by bread alone (Deut. 8:3); and the enjoyment of God's gifts apart from obedience to the word of God is not life.

We must understand the Old Testament concept of man to understand its view of the intermediate state, and we must understand the Old Testament concept of the world to understand its doctrine of man. Just as there is no trace of dualistic thinking about the world, so the Old Testament view of man is not dualistic. Man is not, as the Greeks thought, a dualism of body and soul, or of body and spirit. "Spirit" is God's breath, God's power, working in the world (Isa. 40:7; 31:3). It is God's breath creating and sustaining life (Ps. 33:6; 104:29-30). Man's "spirit" is man's breath which comes from God (Isa. 42:5; Job 33:4; 27:3; 32:8). When God breathed into man the breath of life, man became a living being (literally, "soul," Gen. 2:7). Animals, as well as man, are sustained by the breath of life (Gen. 7:15). Therefore, the basic meaning of "soul" (*nephesh*) in the Old Testament is the principle of life which animates both men (Exod. 21:23; Judg. 5:18; Ps. 33:19) and animals (Prov. 12:10). The meaning of soul — *nephesh* — is then extended to designate man as a person (Gen. 14:21; Exod. 16:16; Num. 5:6; Ezek. 33:6 [RSV, "anyone"]; Deut. 24:7 [RSV, "one"]; Gen. 46:18 [sixteen "persons"]), and is also extended to designate the seat of the appetites and desires, and the self with its emotions and thoughts. Nowhere, however, do body or flesh and soul or spirit represent two parts of men — the lower and the higher.

The Old Testament's concept of existence after death is closely related to its view of man. The soul or spirit does not escape the physical world to flee to the world of God. Rather, man descends to Sheol. Sheol is thought of as a place beneath the earth (Ps. 86:13; Prov. 15:24; Ezek. 26:20), in the depths of the earth (Ps. 63:9; Ezek. 31:14; 32:18). However, Sheol cannot be identified with the grave, for unburied dead are in Sheol (Gen. 37:35). Thus Sheol is seen as synonymous with death — a state rather than a place. It is a state of existence removed from the blessings of God (Eccl. 9:10; Isa. 38:18; Ps. 115:17; 88:12). Consciousness and identity are not destroyed. In Ezekiel 32:17-32, the Egyptians are condemned to go down to the nether world, that is, to be slain in battle, and the inmates of Sheol are pictured as the Assyrians, the Elamites, the Edomites — each people gathered together according to their human relationships. Isaiah 14:9-10 pictures the dead in Sheol rousing themselves to meet the king of Babylon. Those who had been kings of the earth are seen as rising from their thrones to welcome their erstwhile companion.

What is seen in Sheol is not man's soul or spirit but the *rephaim*, translated "shades" in the Revised Standard Version, the "dead" in the King James. "The shades below tremble, the waters and their inhabitants" (Job 26:5). The shades are unable to rise up and praise God (Ps. 88:10). "Sheol beneath is stirred up to meet you when you come, it rouses the shades to greet you, all who were kings of the nations" (Isa. 14:9; see also Prov. 9:18).

The shades are not to be identified with man's departed soul or spirit. It seems to be some kind of a pale replica of man himself. It attests to the Hebrews' conviction, shared with other ancient peoples, that death does not mean the end of human existence. It appears that God has implanted in the hearts of men everywhere the idea that somehow man will survive death.

However, the Hebrew concept of death also witnesses to the conviction that *life is bodily life*. For the shades in Sheol, conscious fellowship with God has been lost; therefore descent to Sheol does not mean life.

In only a few places does the revelation given in the Old

Testament transcend the expectation of existence in Sheol. The Psalmist writes, "For thou wilt not give me up to Sheol, or let thy godly one see the Pit. Thou dost show me the path of life; in thy presence there is fullness of joy, in thy right hand are pleasures for evermore" (Ps. 16:10-11). Here the Psalmist is seized by the conviction that for the godly man who has lived on earth in conscious fellowship with God, Sheol cannot be the last word. He believes that God will show him the path of life which will pass from the underworld into the presence of God when the dead will experience continuing fellowship with God.

Another glimmer of the same hope is found in Psalm 49:15, "But God will ransom my soul from the power of Sheol, for he will receive me." The same thought occurs in Psalm 73:24, "Thou dost guide me with thy counsel, and afterward thou wilt receive me to glory."

However, in the Old Testament life is bodily existence. This is why the doctrine of bodily resurrection is essential to life.

When we turn to the New Testament, the most vivid passage that seems to tell something about the intermediate state is the story of the rich man and Lazarus in Luke 16:19-31. Those who take this as a revelation about existence after death point to the fact that it is not called a parable, and contrary to Jesus' usual custom in parables, a concrete name is given to one of his characters — Lazarus. However, "Lazarus" is the Greek form of a Hebrew word meaning "God has helped" and has the symbolic significance that since the poor man could not trust the rich man, he trusted God, who in turn helped him with the gift of salvation. If this is a true story, it teaches that the intermediate state is divided into two parts — Hades and Abraham's bosom. Hades is the Greek equivalent for the Hebrew Sheol. These two divisions are separated by a great gulf, which did not, however, prevent communication back and forth. It teaches that the wicked in Hades are in torment in flames while the righteous are in blessedness in Abraham's bosom.

However, there is one teaching in this passage which contradicts the total biblical teaching about the intermediate state, namely, that judgment and reward take place immediately after death. Elsewhere judgment always occurs at the Second Coming of Christ. Since this passage reflects ideas about Hades that were current in Judaism, we conclude that this is not meant to be a true story but is a parable based on contemporary ideas. Furthermore, Jesus nowhere teaches that wealth per se deserves hell while poverty deserves heaven. The parable is really not about the poor man and his fate, but about the five brothers. The key line is: "If they do not hear Moses and the prophets, neither will they be convinced if some one should rise from the dead" (16:31). The parable is about the hardness and obduracy of the Jews who refuse to accept the witness of Scripture to the person of Jesus.

The clearest word in the Gospels about the intermediate state — at least of the righteous — is found in Jesus' word to the dying criminal. The thief had been deeply impressed by Jesus' conduct and he finally turned to Jesus with the prayer, "Jesus, remember me when you come in your kingly power" (Lk. 23:42). Apparently the thief had known something about the controversy over Jesus' messiahship, and he concludes that, in spite of the fact that Jesus was crucified, he was indeed the Messiah, and at some undefined day in the future, he would appear as God's anointed to establish his kingdom. In reply Jesus said, "Truly, I say to you, today you will be with me in Paradise" (Lk. 23:43).

"Paradise" is a Greek loan-word from Persian which means "park" or "garden." In the Old Testament it was used of the garden of Eden (Ezek. 28:13; 31:8). In later Jewish writing, it becomes a term designating the blessed abode of the righteous between death and resurrection. Paul refers to Paradise as the dwelling place of God in II Corinthians 12:4. He was caught up in ecstasy so that he caught a glimpse of Paradise. Because the thief has expressed faith in Jesus, he will enjoy fellowship with him

34

in the presence of God "today," that is, immediately after death.

The New Testament nowhere goes beyond this statement that the redeemed enjoy fellowship with Christ in the intermediate state. Paul affirms the same thing, but adds no new light on the state of the dead, when he says that in contrast to the sufferings he has experienced as an apostle, he would prefer "to depart [from this life] and be with Christ, for that is far better" (Phil. 1:23). The reference to the "heavenly kingdom" in II Timothy 4:18 probably points to the same hope.

One passage in Paul is thought by some scholars to throw more light on the intermediate state:

> For we know that if the earthly tent we live in is destroyed, we have a building from God, a house not made with hands, eternal in the heavens. Here [in the body] we groan, and long to put on our heavenly dwelling, so that by putting it on we may not be found naked. For while we are still in this tent [of our earthly body] we sigh with anxiety; not that we would be unclothed, but that we would be further clothed, so that what is mortal may be swallowed up by life. . . . So we are always of good courage; we know that while we are at home in the body we are away from the Lord, for we walk by faith, not by sight. We are of good courage, and we would rather be away from the body and at home with the Lord. So whether we are at home or away, we make it our aim to please him. (II Cor. 5:1-9)

This passage is interpreted in two very different ways by evangelical scholars. Some place emphasis upon the verb: If our earthly body is destroyed in death, *we have* at the moment of death our redeemed bodies, "not made with hands, eternal in the heavens." It is true that in his earlier letters, Paul places the resurrection at the Parousia (Second Coming) of Christ (I Thess. 4). The usual view is that between the writing of First and Second Corinthians, Paul faced the danger of imminent death as he had never done before (II Cor. 6:9) and this led him to reflect on what will happen after death. This in turn led him to change his mind and to conclude that those in Christ would put on their resurrection bodies immediately after death. Therefore II Corinthians 5 is the fullest word in the New Testament about the state of the righteous dead.

There are several difficulties in this view. In the first place, Paul was no stranger to death before he wrote II Corinthians. In I Corinthians 15:31, Paul says, "I die every day"; he is constantly facing the danger of physical death. In the second place, in Philippians 3:20-21, Paul places the transformation of the body at the Second Coming of Christ as he had done in I Thessalonians. There is therefore evidence that he had not changed his mind about the intermediate state.

Finally, if II Corinthians 5 describes a body received at death, it is difficult to see why Paul still thought there was need of a further resurrection at the Parousia of Christ. The body described in II Corinthians strikes the note of eschatological finality: "so that what is mortal may be swallowed up by life" (II Cor. 5:4). However, in Philippians 3:20, written after Corinthians, Paul is clearly expecting the reception of the transformed resurrection body at the Second Advent. "But our commonwealth is in heaven, and from it we await a Savior, the Lord Jesus Christ, who will change our lowly body to be like his glorious body, by the power which enables him even to subject all things to himself."

For these reasons, the more traditional interpretation of II Corinthians 5 still seems preferable. Paul is speaking principally of the resurrection body. Death has lost its terror, for it is not the end of life. On the contrary, we know that we have a body awaiting us — a resurrection body — an eternal body, a heavenly body. The present tense, "we have" a building from God, expresses the certainty of receiving this heavenly body. In Romans 8:30, Paul speaks of the final eschatological event — glorification — in the past tense, so certain is he that he will experience it. "Those whom he called, he also justified, and those whom he justified he also glorified." When this body is received, "that which is mortal [will be] swallowed up by life" (II Cor. 5:4). Paul looks forward to the resurrection because in our earthly existence we groan from weakness, sickness, and suffering, and long to put on our heavenly dwelling. The alternative to the resurrection is "being found naked" — being a disembodied spirit. And even though death has lost its terror, it remains a formidable enemy. Paul does not anticipate with any delight the putting off of the mortal tent, for it means being "unclothed" — without a body; and what he longs for is to be "further clothed [at the resurrection] so that what is mortal may be swallowed up by life" (II Cor. 5:4). In this Paul stands in sharp contrast to Greek dualism which considered the body a hindrance to man's best self and looked forward to attaining to a disembodied, "spiritual" realm. For Paul the resurrection means everything. Apparently he has been given no divine guidance about the state of the dead after death. All he can say is "nakedness."

However, there is one fact which takes the sting out of leaving the body even before receiving the resurrection body. "So we are always of good courage; we know that while we are at home in the body, we are away from the Lord, for we walk by faith, not by sight. We are of good courage [even in the face of disembodiment], and we would rather be away from the body and at home with the Lord" (II Cor. 5:6-8). Here Paul says the same things he says in Philippians 1:23. He knows nothing about the state of the righteous dead, and he shrinks from dying short of the resurrection. But even so death holds no fear, for the dead will be with Christ while they await the resurrection.

In summary, Paul's witness agrees with the word of Jesus to the dying thief. God's people will be with him after death; but the New Testament gives us few details about the nature of the intermediate state.

There is one glimpse of the intermediate state in Hebrews 12:23, where there is a passing reference to "the spirits of just men made perfect." This is probably not a general statement but a specific one, referring to the Old Testament saints. The author has concluded Chapter 11 — his great roll call of Old Testament heroes — by saying, "And all these, though well attested by their faith, did not receive what was promised, since God had forseen something better for us, that apart from us they should not be made perfect" (Heb. 11:39-40). This "perfection" is found in Jesus Christ, "For by a single offering he has perfected for all time those who are sanctified" (Heb. 10:14). "Perfection" by the death of Christ is what the Old Testament sacrificial system could not do — bring men into a living fellowship with God. This has been accomplished *now* for New Testament saints, and it has also been accomplished for the Old Testament saints after their death, for they too were men of faith.

A notoriously difficult passage is found in I Peter 3:19-20: "[in the Spirit] he went and preached to the spirits in prison, who formerly did not obey, when God's patience waited in the days of Noah, during the building of the ark, in which a few, that is, eight persons, were saved through water." This passage has received and still does receive diverse interpretations. We can here do little more than mention the three major interpretations. The older patristic interpretation is that in the intermediate state Christ in the spirit went and preached the gospel to the spirits of dead men imprisoned in Hades who lived either in the days of Noah or in the time before Christ. This view soon lost favor, for it opened the door to the possibility of salvation after death. A second view, held by Augustine and many Reformers, is that Christ in his preexistent state of being preached the gospel through Noah to Noah's living contemporaries. The third view, most widely accepted today, is that in the intermediate state Christ proclaimed the victory of the gospel to fallen angels imprisoned in Hades. The "preaching" involved need not mean an offer of salvation, but the triumphant announcement that through his death and resurrection Christ had broken the power of the spirit world.

This may find some support in Jude 6: "And the angels that did not keep their own position but left their proper dwelling have been kept by him in eternal chains in nether gloom until the judgment of the great day."

Doubtless some interpreters would look to Revelation 6:9 for further light on the intermediate state: "When he opened the fifth seal, I saw under the altar the souls of those who had been slain for the word of God and for the witness they had borne." However, this sheds no light on this question. It is rather a metaphorical way to describe the death of the martyrs and has nothing to say about their dwelling place after death. In the Old Testament, when animals were sacrificed to the Lord, their blood was poured out at the foot of the altar (Lev. 4:7). The souls of the martyrs are seen under the altar in heaven because their lives had been poured out as a sacrificial offering to God. The New Testament often employs the language of sacrificial death. Facing death, the apostle Paul wrote, "For I am already on the point of being sacrificed" (II Tim. 4:6). At an earlier date he had written, "For if I am to be poured as a libation upon the sacrificial offering of your faith, I am glad" (Phil. 2:17). The Christian martyrs in the Revelation are viewed as sacrifices offered to God. In fact, they were slain on earth, and their blood wet the ground; but in Christian faith the sacrifice was really made in heaven where their souls — their lives — were offered at the heavenly altar.

In summary, the New Testament has very little to say about the intermediate state. In fact, it sheds no light on the state of the unrighteous dead. The one fact that is taught by both the Gospels and Paul is that the righteous dead — believers — are with Christ in the presence of God, awaiting the resurrection. While this is a state of blessedness, the entire Bible witnesses to the fact that the final redemption must include the resurrection and transformation of the body.

IV

THE SECOND COMING OF CHRIST

TO UNDERSTAND THE SIGNIFICANCE OF THE SECOND COMING OF Christ in the New Testament, one needs an over-all view of the basic nature of biblical theology. The Bible everywhere assumes the reality of the visible, natural world, but it equally assumes the existence of an invisible, spiritual world — the dwelling place of God. "Now faith is the assurance of things hoped for, *the conviction of things not seen*" (Heb. 11:1). This world is imperceptible to the physical senses. It can be apprehended only by faith. The Bible nowhere tries to prove the reality of this unseen world; it is everywhere taken for granted, even as the existence of God himself is assumed: "For whoever would draw near to God must *believe* that he exists and that he rewards those who seek him" (Heb. 11:6).

This dualism of God *vs.* the world may seem to be very similar to the Greek dualism mentioned in the preceding chapter, of the spiritual *vs.* the material world. But the similarity is in reality superficial. There is a profound difference between Greek and Hebrew dualism. Greek dualism, as has already been pointed out, claims a parallel body-soul dualism in man. Man in his body belongs to the material world, but in his soul — wherein lies his true and most real life — he belongs to the invisible spiritual world. Therefore the wise man is he who cultivates his soul and strictly controls his body so it does not interfere with his soul. At death the wise man will escape from the visible world of matter and take his flight to the invisible spiritual world. "Salvation" means escape from the body which is the tomb of the soul.

Hebrew dualism is very different. While it realizes that something has gone wrong in the natural world, it continues to assert that this world in its essence is good and never evil. Man's natural dwelling is the earth. He knows God not by the discipline of bodily appetites and cultivation of the soul, but by God coming to man in his earthly, historical existence.

In Greek thought man flees the world to God; in Hebrew thought God comes down to man. Furthermore, God is to be known by his visitations of man in history in which he reveals himself. The greatest revelatory act of God in the Old Testament was the divine visitations of God in Egypt to deliver Israel and constitute them his people. The Exodus was no ordinary event in history like the events which befell other nations. It was not an achievement of the Israelites. It was not attributed to the genius and skillful leadership of Moses. It was an act of God. "You have seen what I did to the Egyptians, and how I bore you on eagles' wings" (Exod. 19:4). Nor was this deliverance merely an act of God; it was an act through which Israel was to know and serve God. "I am the Lord, and I will bring you out from under the burdens of the Egyptians, and I will deliver you from their bondage, and *you shall know that I am the Lord your God*" (Exod. 6:6-7).

In the later history of Israel the Exodus is recited again and again as the redemptive act by which God made himself known to his people. Hosea appeals to Israel's historical redemption and subsequent experiences as evidence of the love of God. "When Israel was a child, I loved him, and out of Egypt I called my son.... I led them with cords of compassion, with the bands of love" (Hos. 11:1,4).

History also reveals God in wrath and judgment. Hosea goes on immediately to say that Israel is about to return

41

to captivity because of her sins. Amos interprets Israel's impending historical destruction with the words, "Therefore thus I will do to you, O Israel; because I will do this to you, prepare to meet your God, O Israel!" (Amos 4:12). The revelation of God as judge of his people in historical events is sharply reflected in the designation of Israel's historical defeat by the Assyrians as the "day of the Lord."

These wonderful visitations of God in the past are sometimes described in terms of what the theologian calls a theophany — an appearance of God. Before the glory and majesty of the divine visitation, creation is shaken.

The mountains saw thee, and writhed. . . .
The sun and the moon stood still in their habitation. . . .
Thou didst bestride the earth in fury,
  thou didst trample the nations in anger.
Thou wentest forth for the salvation of thy people,
  for the salvation of thy anointed.
                                    (Hab. 3:10, 11, 12-13)

We have seen in an earlier chapter that there are three different messianic personages in the Old Testament — the Davidic Messiah, the heavenly Son of Man, and the Suffering Servant who will be instrumental in the final eschatological salvation of God's people.

It is often overlooked that frequently the Old Testament looks forward to the eschatological visitation in terms of a theophany, an appearance of the glory and majesty of God in the face of which creation will shudder and shake. One should read all of Isaiah 24-25 to appreciate this; here we can cite only a few verses.

Behold the Lord will lay waste the earth and make it
    desolate, and he will twist its surface and scatter its
    inhabitants. . . .
The earth shall be utterly laid waste and utterly despoiled,
    for the Lord has spoken this word. . . .
On that day the Lord will punish the host of heaven in
    heaven, and the kings of the earth, on the earth,
They will be gathered together as prisoners in a pit;
        they will be shut up in a prison, and after many days
        they will be punished.

THE SECOND COMING OF CHRIST

Then the moon will be confounded, and the sun ashamed;
for the Lord of hosts will reign on Mount Zion and in
Jerusalem,
and before his elders he will manifest his glory.
(Isa. 24:1, 3, 21-23)

The important line is "The Lord of hosts will reign in Mount Zion." The establishment of God's rule, his Kingdom, is the central hope of the prophets. It will mean three things: the shaking and judgment of a fallen creation, the punishment of the wicked, and the salvation of God's people in a renewed earth. The same passage in Isaiah goes on to say:

> On this mountain the Lord of hosts will make for all peoples a feast of fat things, a feast of wine on the lees, of fat things full of marrow, of wine on the lees well refined. . . . He will swallow up death forever, and the Lord will wipe away tears from all faces, and the reproach of his people he will take away from all the earth; for the Lord has spoken. (Isa. 25:6, 8).

This same theology of eschatological theophany, of the visitation of God to judge the earth and mankind and to redeem his people, will be found in such passages as Joel 3:14-21 and Zephaniah 2, which we cannot here take space to quote. The important fact in such passages is that God will yet visit mankind in history, in his earthly existence, for both judgment and salvation. Nowhere is salvation conceived of as a flight from history as in Greek thought; it is always the coming of God to man in history. Man does not ascend to God; God descends to man. History is not the stage on which man lives out his human existence only to leave it; history shares with man both judgment and salvation.

In the New Testament this theology of the coming of God takes a new and unforeseen form—incarnation. Jesus of Nazareth was a man endowed with supernatural powers. Practically all of modern scholarship, both evangelical and liberal, admits that Jesus performed what appeared to be miracles of healing. One of the most characteristic

43

miracles of Jesus was the exorcism of demons. Many modern men do not know what to do with the gospel teaching about demon-possession, but it is clear that it is an inextricable strand in the ministry of Jesus. Indeed, from one point of view it may be considered the most central strand.

At Jesus' baptism the voice from heaven proclaimed Jesus as the Son of God, as the Elect One. Election is involved in the words "with whom I am well pleased" (Matt. 3:17). The baptism is followed immediately by the temptation, which must be understood in light of the baptism. The threefold temptation assumes that Jesus is the Son of God: "If you are the Son of God [as you think you are]" (Matt. 4:3). The heart of the temptation was to persuade Jesus to abandon God's will in carrying out his messianic mission. "If you are the Son of God, display your deity by jumping down from the wing of the temple without injury and thus awe the crowds into worshipping you." The temptation marks the beginning of a struggle between Jesus and the powers of Satan which continued throughout his ministry.

On one occasion after Jesus had exorcised a demon, the leaders of the Jews admitted that Jesus had supernatural power but this power was Satanic — the power of Beelzebul. Jesus replied that such a state of affairs was impossible, for it would mean civil war in the domain of Satan and thus lead to his ruin. Then Jesus said, "But if it is by the Spirit of God that I cast out demons, then the kingdom of God has come upon you. Or how can one enter a strong man's house and plunder his goods, unless he first binds the strong man? Then indeed he may plunder his house" (Matt. 12:28-29). It was Jesus' earthly mission to deliver man from Satanic power. This meant "invading" the strong man's house — this world — to "plunder his goods," to wrest men and women from Satanic power. The most obvious symbol of this was deliverance from demon possession. Jesus had wrestled with Satan and had "bound" him, had conquered him so that he had to release his erstwhile slaves.

44

Demon exorcism was only the negative side of receiving into one's life the power of God's kingly rule. Demon exorcism was not an end in itself; the life must be filled with the power of God. Otherwise the demon can return, and the final situation will be worse than the first. The victorious conquest of Satan is further illustrated in the preaching mission of the seventy disciples. Returning from their mission, they reported that even the demons were subject to them in Jesus' name. Jesus replied, "I saw Satan fall like lightning from heaven" (Luke 10:18). This is clearly symbolic language and not meant to be a geographical or astronomical statement. In the mission of the seventy disciples Jesus saw Satan toppled from his place of power. The binding of Satan, his falling from heaven, are both metaphorical ways of stating that Satan has been defeated in his struggle with Jesus.

The Gospel of John adds something which is only implicit in the first three Gospels. It speaks clearly of the preexistence and incarnation of Christ. "In the beginning was the Word and the Word was with God, and the Word was God. . . . And the Word became flesh and dwelt among us" (John 1:1, 14). Paul witnesses to the same truth. "Though he [Christ] was in the form of God, [he] did not count equality with God a thing to be grasped, but emptied himself, taking the form of a servant, being born in the likeness of men. And being found in human form, he humbled himself and became obedient unto death, even death on a cross" (Phil. 2:6-8). In other words, the story of Jesus of Nazareth is not the story of a religious genius, a far-sighted prophet, an unusually endowed man. It is all this, but more. It is the story of incarnation, of enfleshment, of the visitation of men by the God of heaven. "His name shall be called Emmanuel (which means, God with us)" (Matt. 1:23). Modern scholarship has been in search of "the historical Jesus," a Jesus who is no bigger than history, who can be understood in thoroughly human terms. But no "historical Jesus" has been found which satisfies the gospel portrait. To say "Jesus" means to say

45

"God." This is why Jesus could say, "He who has seen me has seen the Father" (John 14:9).

And yet Jesus is not the incarnation of unveiled deity. "The Word became *flesh*." Deity was veiled in human flesh. "He emptied himself [of his glory], taking the form of a servant." Jesus made little impression on some people because they had known him from boyhood. "Is this not Jesus, the son of Joseph, whose father and mother we know?" (John 6:42). As we have pointed out in an earlier chapter, Jesus had the messianic mission to fulfill the role of the Suffering Servant before he should be the Son of Man in glory. The point we are now making is that, contrary to outward appearances, the life of Jesus of Nazareth embodies an invasion into history by God, veiled though it was. In this veiled form the presence of God could be seen only by the eyes of faith. After the miracle of transforming the water into wine at Cana of Galilee, according to John, Jesus manifested his glory (John 2:11). This was not evident to everyone, only to believing disciples. Most of the people experienced only extra fine wine.

We have pointed out that it was part of the main mission of Jesus to overthrow the power of Satan. Paul sees this as being accomplished also by Jesus' death and resurrection. "He disarmed the principalities and powers and made a public example of them, triumphing over them in him" (Col. 2:15). One of the main motifs in the New Testament as to the meaning of Jesus' resurrection and ascension is his victory over the powers of evil. On the day of Pentecost, Peter sounded this note. "The Lord [God] said to my Lord [Messiah], Sit at my right hand, till I make thy enemies a stool for thy feet" (Acts 2:34). Christ has already rendered Satan a decisive defeat; but Satan is not yet destroyed. "For he [Christ] must reign [as King and Messiah] until he has put all his enemies under his feet. The last enemy to be destroyed is death" (I Cor. 15:25-26).

This touches on the theology of the Kingdom of God. Jesus is finally to "deliver the kingdom to God the Father after destroying every rule and every authority and power" (I Cor. 15:24). The Kingdom of God is God's rule, manifested in Christ. We have already seen that Jesus' act of exorcising demons — of delivering men and women from Satanic power — was the outward evidence that the Kingdom of God *has come* to men in history (Matt. 12:28). In his resurrection and exaltation he was enthroned at the right hand of God (Acts 2:34-36). He is even now reigning as messianic King. Men and women continue to be delivered from bondage to darkness and transferred into the Kingdom of Christ (Col. 1:13). But the world does not know it. The world goes on as though Jesus had never come, as though the Kingdom of God was merely a dream. There are indeed millions of Christian believers in the world today who express his Lordship, who seek the ways of peace and righteousness. But they are not enough to mold the course of nations. Jesus himself said that there would be disturbances, wars, evils, and persecutions throughout the course of the age. The presence of God's Kingdom in the historical mission of Jesus was primarily a spiritual event. Although he has been defeated, Satan and the powers of evil are still very much with us. The world is still an evil place. The nations of the world ignore God and his Kingdom.

This is why the Second Coming of Christ is necessary — to complete the work begun in his Incarnation. There are, in other words, two great events in God's conquest of the powers of evil, two invasions of God into history: the Incarnation and the Second Coming. One scholar has illustrated this by an analogy from World War II. There were two steps in the victory over Nazi Germany: D-Day and V-Day. Once the allies had launched a successful invasion upon the continent and the allied armies had secured a foothold and started their drive across France, the tide of battle turned. The allies were advancing, Germany was in retreat. But there remained much bitter fighting, which lasted until the complete capitulation of the enemy — V-Day. Then the fighting ceased; peace reigned.

So Jesus has invaded the realm of Satan and rendered him a decisive defeat. Because of Jesus' victory in his life, death, and exaltation, the tide of battle has turned. Since Pentecost the gospel of the Kingdom of God has been preached in nearly all the world, and an ever increasing multitude of men and women are rescued from the dominion of Satan and brought under the reign of Christ. An ever enlarging number of people bow before the Lordship of Christ. But he must reign until "every enemy is put beneath his feet" (I Cor. 15:25). Since these enemies are spiritual enemies — Satanic enemies — this is a victory that neither men nor the church can win. It can only be done by a direct act of God. The power that was in the incarnate Jesus in hidden and veiled form will be manifested in power and glory.

Another way of looking at the same fact: Jesus *is* now the Lord; he is enthroned at the right hand of God; he is reigning in his Kingdom. But this is a Lordship and a kingly reign which is known only to believers. It must be confessed by faith. His Second Coming will mean nothing less than the Lordship which is his now will be made visible to all the world. When we pray, "Thy kingdom come," this is what we are praying for: the effectual and universal rule of Christ in all the world, not only over believers. Then, when his Kingdom comes, "at the name of Jesus every knee [shall] bow, in heaven and on earth and under the earth, and every tongue confess that Jesus Christ is Lord, to the glory of God the Father" (Phil. 2:10-11).

The eschatological theophany of the Old Testament — the glorious appearing of God — which will establish God's universal rule, is in the New Testament reinterpreted in terms of the Second Coming of Christ. He will come as the heavenly Son of Man and bring his Kingdom to his saints. He will reign in his Kingdom as the messianic King.

V

THE LANGUAGE OF THE SECOND ADVENT

WE MUST NOW DEAL WITH A QUESTION THAT HAS BECOME A subject of tragic controversy in many evangelical churches. Dispensationalism, which we discussed in the first chapter, has taught that there will be two comings of Christ, or rather, that the Second Coming of Christ will occur in two stages. We have seen that Dispensationalism teaches that there are two peoples of God — Israel and the church — and that God has two different programs — one for Israel and one for the church. The program for Israel is an earthly, theocratic program; the program for the church is a spiritual, heavenly program. Corresponding to this are two phases in the Second Coming of Christ. The Bible teaches, as we shall see in the next chapter, that the struggle between the Kingdom of God and the power of Satan will come to its climax in a brief but terrible struggle between Satan and the church, where the devil will try to turn all men away from Christ. This will be a time of fearful martyrdom; it is called the Great Tribulation (Matt. 24:21; Rev. 7:14). Dispensationalists hold that Christ will come before the Tribulation begins to raise the dead saints and to catch up the living saints (the Rapture) to be with him in heaven. Thus the church will escape the Great Tribulation; the persecution against the "saints" will be directed against Israel — the living Jews. At the end of the Tribulation Christ will return, this time accompanied by the church (I Thess. 3:13), to rescue Israel

49

and to bring them into his millennial Kingdom. These two comings of Christ have been called the Rapture — when he comes to catch up the church — and the Revelation. The Rapture will be a secret coming, known only by the church. The Revelation will be a public, visible coming where he comes with power and glory to establish his Kingdom.

This pretribulation coming of Christ to raise the dead saints and to rapture the living church has become the most characteristic doctrine of Dispensationalists. We must examine the language used in the New Testament to see if it supports this idea of a coming of Christ before the Great Tribulation.

Three words are employed in the New Testament to describe the second advent. The first is "parousia," which means "coming," "arrival," or "presence." This is the word most frequently used of our Lord's return, and it is used in connection with the Rapture of the church.

> We that are alive, that are left unto the parousia of the Lord, shall in no wise precede them that are fallen asleep. For the Lord himself shall descend from heaven, with a shout, with the voice of the archangel, and with the trump of God; and the dead in Christ shall rise first: then we that are alive, that are left, shall together with them be caught up in the clouds to meet the Lord in the air; and so shall we ever be with the Lord. (I Thess. 4:15-17)

It is very difficult to find a secret coming of Christ in these verses. His coming will be attended with a shout, with the voice of the archangel, and with the heavenly trumpet. Someone has said that the shout and the trumpet sound will be loud enough to wake the dead!

Furthermore, the parousia of Christ will occur not only to rapture the church and to raise the righteous dead but also to destroy the Man of Lawlessness, the Antichrist. "And then shall be revealed the lawless one, whom the Lord Jesus shall slay with the breath of his mouth, and bring to naught by the manifestation of his parousia" (II Thess. 2:8). This is obviously no secret event, for the parousia of Christ will be an outshining, a manifestation. Furthermore, this verse locates the parousia at the end of the Tribulation. One would naturally conclude by comparing the verses just cited that the Rapture of the living saints, the resurrection of those who have died, and the judgment upon the Antichrist will all take place at the same time, namely, at the parousia of Jesus at the end of Tribulation.

Furthermore, it is at his parousia that Jesus will be accompanied by all his saints. Paul prays that God may establish the Thessalonians in holiness "at the parousia of our Lord Jesus with all his saints" (I Thess. 3:13). At his parousia the Lord will come to bring his saints with him, to raise the righteous dead, to rapture the living believers, and to destroy Antichrist.

The parousia will be a glorious event. Christ will destroy the Man of Lawlessness by the breath of his mouth and "by the manifestation [literally, "epiphany" or "outshining"] of his parousia" (II Thess. 2:8). The rendition of the King James Version is not wrong: "by the brightness of his coming." This epiphany will be a glorious event, for Paul speaks of "the epiphany of the glory of our great God and our Saviour" (Titus 2:13).

We find the same teaching of a glorious visible parousia in Jesus' words. "For as the lightning cometh forth from the east, and is seen even unto the west; so shall be the parousia of the Son of man" (Matt. 24:27). It will be like a bolt of lightning, glorious, visible, evident to all.

The usual answer given to these facts by those who separate the coming of Christ into two parts is that parousia means "presence" and therefore covers the entire period of time which is introduced by the Rapture and the beginning of the Tribulation. Thus, we are told, parousia can refer either to the coming of Christ at the Rapture or to his Revelation at the end of the Tribulation.

It is true that sometimes parousia does mean "presence." Paul contrasts his presence (parousia) with the Philippians with his absence (apousia) from them (Phil. 2:12). The

51

Corinthians accused Paul of inconsistency, because "his letters . . . are strong, but his bodily presence is weak" (II Cor. 10:10). However, the word does not always mean "presence"; more often it means "arrival." When Paul in Ephesus received envoys from Corinth, he rejoiced at their parousia, that is, their coming or arrival (I Cor. 16:17). When Paul was concerned about the condition of things at Corinth, he was comforted by the arrival (parousia) of Titus (II Cor. 7:6). It was not the presence of Titus but his arrival with good news from Corinth that provided the comfort. To translate parousia by "presence" would empty it of its particular point. This is illustrated in the following instances: "Be patient, brethren, until the parousia of the Lord. . . . Be ye also patient; establish your hearts; for the parousia of the Lord is at hand" (Jas. 5:7-8). "Where is the promise of his parousia?" (II Pet. 3:4). In these verses it is the coming, the return, the advent of the Lord which is called for; "presence" does not suit the context.

It is not the presence so much as the coming of Christ which is required in the verses we have just discussed. It is at the coming, the advent of Christ, that the dead will be raised and the living caught up; "presence" does not fit. It is at his coming, his advent, not his presence, that he will be accompanied by his saints. His coming, his advent, will be like a bolt of lightning. The parousia of Christ is his second coming, and it will bring both salvation and judgment: salvation of the saints, and judgment of the world.

A second word used of our Lord's return is *apokalypsis,* which means "revelation." The apocalypse or Revelation of Christ is distinguished by pretribulationists from the Rapture of the church and is placed at the end of the Tribulation when Christ comes in glory to bring judgment upon the world. If this view is correct, then *the apocalypse of Christ is not primarily the blessed hope of the Christian.* When the Revelation occurs, the saints will have been raptured and will have received from the hand of Christ their rewards for the things done in the body. They will already have entered into the full enjoyment of life and fellowship with Christ. The apocalypse of Christ is for judgment of the wicked, not for the salvation of the church. According to pretribulationism, the Rapture at the secret coming of Christ is our blessed hope and the object of our fond expectation, not the Revelation.

This, however, is not what we find in the Scripture. We are *"waiting for* the revelation of our Lord Jesus Christ" (I Cor. 1:7). According to pretribulationism we are not waiting for the Revelation but for the Rapture. The church is to suffer affliction until the time of the apocalypse of Christ. Paul says that "it is a righteous thing with God to recompense affliction to them that afflict you, and to you that are afflicted, rest with us, at the revelation of the Lord Jesus Christ from heaven, with the angels of his power in flaming fire" (II Thess. 1:6-7). According to pretribulationism this rest from persecution has already been experienced at the Rapture; it does not await the Revelation of Jesus Christ. But the Word of God says it is received at the Revelation.

It has recently been argued that the expression in the Greek does not mean "when the Lord Jesus shall be revealed," but "in the revelation of the Lord Jesus," that is, not the moment when Christ is revealed but the period of time during which his revelation occurs. When Christ is revealed, the afflicted will already be enjoying rest. This, however, is a very unnatural interpretation of Paul's language. Let us take note of the full expression: "if indeed it is a righteous thing with God to recompense . . . to you who are afflicted, rest with us, in the revelation of the Lord Jesus." The verb "to recompense" controls two objects: (1) affliction to those who afflict you, and (2) rest to you who are afflicted. Both the recompense of affliction and of rest will be "in the revelation of the Lord." If affliction is to be given when Christ is revealed, then the rest must also be given when Christ is revealed. To say that the rest has already been received and is being enjoyed

53

is imposing upon the verse an assumption which is controverted by the wording of the passage.

Peter employs the same expression. Now we are partakers of the sufferings of Christ, that "at the revelation of his glory also ye may rejoice with exceeding joy" (I Pet. 4:13). This suggests that the fiery trial will be terminated only at the apocalypse of Christ. Furthermore, Peter says that the genuineness of our faith will bring "praise and glory and honor at the revelation of Jesus Christ" (I Pet. 1:7). According to pretribulationism this glory and honor has already been experienced at an earlier time at the Rapture of the church. This verse, however, asserts that one of the purposes of the apocalypse of Christ is to bring to his people glory and honor because of their steadfastness in their faith. Finally, Peter assures us that our hope of the perfection in grace will be brought unto us at the Revelation of Jesus Christ. If these two events are one and the same, these verses are full of meaning. If, however, these blessings are not received at the Revelation but at an earlier Rapture, these verses are quite perplexing and difficult. It is difficult to see how a distinction can be made between these two events. The Revelation is continually made the object of our hope; the Rapture must therefore occur at the Revelation of Christ. The Scripture nowhere asserts that there is a Rapture which will take place before the Revelation.

The third word which is used of Christ's second coming is *epiphaneia*, which means "manifestation" and must therefore, according to the pretribulation scheme, refer not to the Rapture of the church and a secret coming of Christ at the beginning of the Tribulation but to the Revelation of Christ with his saints at the end of the Tribulation to bring judgment upon the world. It is indeed used in this latter meaning, for Christ will slay the man of lawlessness by the "epiphany of his parousia" (II Thess. 2:8). It is clear that his epiphany will occur at the end of the Tribulation.

This epiphany of Christ is, however, like his apocalypse

the object of the believer's hope, as it could not be if the church had received the object of its hope at an earlier time at the Rapture. Paul exhorts us to keep the commandment without spot and without reproach "until the epiphany of our Lord Jesus Christ" (I Tim. 6:14). At the end of his life Paul expressed confidence that he had fought a good fight, and looking forward to the day of rewards at the judgment seat of Christ, he says, "henceforth there is laid up for me a crown of righteousness which the Lord the righteous judge shall give me at that day; and not to me only, but also to all them that have loved his epiphany" (II Tim. 4:8). One can only conclude from a passage such as this that "that day" which Paul anticipates as a day of rewards is the day of Christ's epiphany. It is therefore a day upon which Christians have set their affection, the object of Christian hope. And it is the day of giving rewards to believers. Pretribulationism places the judgment of rewards *between* the Rapture and the Revelation. Here, it is located at the epiphany, which is the same as the Revelation, at the end of the Tribulation.

This line of thought is clinched by Titus 2:13 and 14: "looking for the blessed hope and the *epiphany* of the glory of the great God and Saviour Jesus Christ; who gave himself for us, that he might redeem us from all iniquity and purify unto himself a people for his own possession, zealous for good works." The blessed hope of the church is the epiphany of the glory of our God and Savior Jesus Christ.

If the Rapture of the church, when we are caught up to meet Christ in the air, is separated by a considerable period of time from his apocalypse and his epiphany, then this is strange language indeed. For according to pretribulationism the coming of Christ at the end of the Tribulation has nothing to do with the reward of his saints or with the salvation of the righteous. The dead have already been raised and the living translated into their resurrection bodies. The judgment of works is now past and the rewards of Christ to his faithful servants have been distributed. The apocalypse and the epiphany of Christ at the end of the Tribulation have as their object judgment and not salvation. Yet according to the Word of God, this epiphany is our blessed hope; it is the time when we shall be rewarded; it is the time when we shall be redeemed from all iniquity and purified to become God's perfect possession; it is the blessed hope of perfect union in fellowship with Christ. Does it not seem then that the Rapture of the church is to take place at the epiphany, not seven years earlier?

Certainly if one can make anything of language at all, no distinction can be made between the parousia, the apocalypse, and the epiphany of our Lord. They are one and the same event. Furthermore, as we have already indicated, although it is argued that the parousia means "presence" and therefore covers the entire period of time introduced by his coming to rapture the church, it is clear from Scripture's use of the words "apocalypse" and "epiphany" that the Revelation of Christ is not an event which has to do exclusively with judgment. *It is also the day upon which the believer's hope is set when he will enter into the completed blessings of salvation at Christ's second coming.*

We can only conclude that the distinction between the Rapture of the church and the Revelation of Christ is an inference which is nowhere asserted by the Word of God and not required by the terminology relating to the return of Christ. On the contrary, if any inference is to be drawn, the terminology suggests that the Revelation of Christ is, like the Rapture, the day of the believer's salvation when he enters into consummated fellowship with the Lord and receives his reward from the hand of the Lord. The parousia, the apocalypse, and the epiphany appear to be a single event. Any division of Christ's coming into two parts is an unproven inference.

The fact that even pretribulationists feel some embarrassment in trying to separate the Second Coming of

Christ into two events or even into two separate parts may be seen in the contention of one of the most recent writers of this school who maintains that the return of Christ for his church is not the Second Coming of Christ. This view makes a distinction between the *return* of Christ and his *second coming*. This is an utterly unwarranted distinction. No support is sought for it in the words used to describe Christ's return. The words "return" and "second coming" are not properly speaking biblical words in that the two words do not represent any equivalent Greek words. There is no difference in the concepts conveyed to the mind by "return" and "coming." It is in other words an artificial and impossible distinction. Christ's parousia is his return; his return is his coming; his coming is his second advent.

The vocabulary used of our Lord's return lends no support for the idea of two comings of Christ or of two aspects of his coming. On the contrary, it substantiates the view that the return of Christ will be a single, indivisible, glorious event.

VI

THE ANTICHRIST AND THE GREAT TRIBULATION

WE HAVE SEEN THAT AT THE HEART OF OUR LORD'S MINISTRY was a fierce struggle between himself and the powers of Satan. In the Olivet discourse Jesus made it clear that his disciples would be exposed to the demonic evil that plagues this age. Even though Jesus had rendered Satan a decisive defeat, the Kingdom of God would not conquer the kingdom of Satan until the Second Coming of Christ. Indeed, in spite of the fact that God had invaded history in Christ, and in spite of the fact that it was to be the mission of Jesus' disciples to evangelize the entire world (Matt. 24:14), the world would remain an evil place. False christs would arise who would lead many astray. Wars, strife, and persecution would continue. Wickedness would abound so as to chill the love of many. In fact, the conflict between the kingdoms of God and of Satan would reach a convulsive end in the appearance of Antichrist at the end of the age.

The idea of Antichrist first appears clearly in the Bible in the book of Daniel. The coming of Antichrist was foreshadowed in a series of events which occurred in 168 B.C. After the return of the Jews from Babylon Israel became a buffer state between Egypt to the south and Syria to the north. Both the Ptolemies of Egypt and the Seleucids of Syria were Greek, stemming from Alexander the Great. In 168 B.C. Palestine was under the rule of the Syrian Seleucids. Their king, Antiochus Epiphanes, decided on a drastic course in trying to assimilate the Jews into his Hellenistic culture. He sent emissaries throughout the land to proclaim that the Jewish religion was to be proscribed, copies of the Old Testament were to be destroyed, a pig sacrificed on the great altar in the Jerusalem temple, and the temple re-dedicated to a Greek god. 1 Maccabees gives us a vivid account of those events, and speaks of the defiling of the temple altar as the abomination of desolation of Daniel.

Daniel 11 reflects these events. Verses 3-4 refer to Alexander the Great and the division of his kingdom into four parts. Verses 5-20 refer to the wars between the kings of the south (Egypt) and of the north (Syria) for dominion of the Holy Land. Verses 21-35 refer to the rise of Antiochus Epiphanes and his persecution of the Jews.

However, in verse 36 there appears to be a change in subject that looks beyond Antiochus to the Antichrist himself, of whom Antiochus was a type. "And the king shall do according to his will; he shall exalt himself above every god, and shall speak astonishing things against the God of gods" (11:36). This goes beyond anything Antiochus did; he tried only to turn the Jews into worshippers of his Greek gods. But the Antichrist "shall give no heed to the god of his fathers . . . he shall not give heed to any other god, for he shall magnify himself above all" (11:37). Here is disclosed the basic character of Antichrist; he arrogates to himself all divine power and "rewards" the worship of men.

The idea of Antichrist also appears in Daniel 7:25: "He shall speak words against the Most High, and shall wear out the saints of the Most High."

Before we leave Daniel, we should examine a passage which is one of the favorite passages for the Dispensational theology of Antichrist. This is the famous passage in Daniel 9:24-27. The important verse is 27:

> Seventy weeks of years are decreed concerning your people and your holy city, to finish the transgression, to put an end to sin, and to atone for iniquity, to bring in

everlasting righteousness, to seal both vision and prophet, and to anoint a most holy place. Know therefore and understand that from the going forth of the word to restore and build Jerusalem to the coming of an anointed one, a prince, there shall be seven weeks. Then for sixty-two weeks it shall be built again with squares and moat, but in a troubled time. And after the sixty-two weeks, an anointed one shall be cut off, and shall have nothing; and the people of the prince who is to come shall destroy the city and the sanctuary. Its end shall come with a flood, and to the end there shall be war; desolations are decreed. And he shall make a strong covenant with many for one week; and for half of the week he shall cause sacrifice and offering to cease; and upon the wing of abominations shall come one who makes desolate, until the decreed end is poured out on the desolator. (Dan. 9:24-27)

This is interpreted by Dispensationalists in terms of Antichrist and his relations with Israel. It is assumed that Israel has returned to Palestine as a nation, has rebuilt the temple, and reinstituted the sacrificial system. Antichrist makes a covenant with Israel which is to last seven years (a week is thought to be seven days of years), but in the midst of the seven years he will break his covenant, disrupt the sacrifices in Jerusalem, and launch a terrible persecution against the Jewish people. This passage with its Dispensational interpretation is foundational to that system of eschatology.

However, it is not at all clear that this interpretation is correct. Many evangelical scholars believe that the messianic interpretation fits the language better than the eschatological one. It discloses God's redemptive purpose "to finish the transgression," that is, to seal up and put away sin as though it no longer had any existence; "to put an end to sin, and to atone for iniquity," that is, Jesus' death on the cross; "to bring in everlasting righteousness," that is, righteousness as the gift of God through the death of his Son; "to seal both vision and prophet," that is, Jesus' bringing of the Old Testament era to an end; "to anoint a most holy place," that is, the anointing of the Messiah with the Spirit of God.

There is every reason to understand the cutting off of an anointed one in verse 26 to refer to the death of Christ and his utter rejection. The verse goes on to describe the fate of the city at the time of Messiah's death. "The people of the prince who is to come shall destroy the city and the sanctuary" may well refer to the utter destruction of Jerusalem and its temple in 70 A.D. by Titus Vespasian, who later became the emperor of Rome. "To the end" of the destruction, war and desolation will continue.

The words in verse 27, "and he shall make a strong covenant with many for a week," are without a subject. Dispensationalists see the subject as Antichrist. However, the language of the Hebrew text is not the usual language implying a covenant. Literally translated it should read, "He shall cause the covenant to prevail." The messianic interpretation sees the subject as Christ, who confirms and fulfills the covenant already in existence so that its terms and conditions are now to be made more effective. This is the covenant in Jesus' blood which fulfills the covenant made with Abraham (Gal. 3:17). By his death he "shall cause sacrifice and offering to cease": his death will put an end to the Jewish sacrificial system (see Heb. 8:13). As a result or consequence of the death of Messiah, one making desolate (the Roman prince, Titus) appears upon the wing of abominations. The "wing" is the pinnacle of the temple (Luke 4:9); the temple itself, which, following the rending of the veil (Mark 15:38), will no longer have any place in the divine plan (Heb. 10:8-18) and will become abominable and unacceptable to the Lord. By this language the complete destruction of the temple is signified. This state of destruction will continue even until the consummation or "full end," which has been determined by God, has been poured out upon the desolate (that is, the ruins of the temple and Jerusalem).

When we turn to the New Testament, we first meet the Antichrist idea in the Olivet discourse, recorded in Matthew 24, Mark 13, and Luke 21. For our present purpose we will limit our discussion largely to Matthew.

The disciples ask Jesus when the temple is to be destroyed and what will be the sign of his Second Coming and the end of the age. Matthew limits himself largely to the first question; Luke is more interested in the destruction of Jerusalem by the Roman armies (see Luke 21:20). But even as in Daniel, where the appearance of the Greek king Antiochus Epiphanes is a type of the eschatological Antichrist, so the coming of the Roman armies under Titus to raze the temple is also a type of the eschatological Antichrist.

Matthew 24 is divided into three parts; verses 3-14 describe the character of the age down to its end. The main theme is that the Kingdom of God will not be established before the Second Coming of Christ. Wars, famines, earthquakes, messianic pretenders will mark the course of the age. As we have already seen, this age is a present evil age (Gal. 1:4); Satan is its god (II Cor. 4:4). However, such events are not meant to be signs by which one can calculate the nearness of the end. In fact, these signs will be seen, "but the end is not yet" (Matt. 24:6). These evils will be "but the beginning of the sufferings" (Matt. 24:8).

In addition to evils which will characterize the age, Jesus' disciples will experience persecution. "There they will deliver you up to tribulation and put you to death; and you will be hated by all nations for my name's sake" (Matt. 24:9). The follower of Jesus is to expect the same treatment that Jesus received. "A disciple is not above his teacher, nor a servant above his master; it is enough for the disciple to be like his teacher, and the servant like his master. If they have called the master of the house Beelzebul, how much more will they malign those of his household" (Matt. 10:24-25). "In the world you have tribulation; but be of good cheer, I have overcome the world" (John 16:33).

However, the age will not be one of unrelieved evil. "This gospel of the kingdom will be preached throughout the whole world, as a testimony to all nations; and then the end will come" (Matt. 24:14). Throughout the world with its evils and hostility the disciples of Jesus are to herald the good news that the Kingdom of God has come (Matt. 12:28), and is yet to come in power and glory.

Some Bible teachers tell us that this verse does not belong to the church but to the saved Jewish remnant in the time of Great Tribulation. Such a view, however, is *read into* the text; it is not found in the text.

In verses 15-28, Jesus speaks of the events that will accompany the end. First he speaks of Antichrist in very difficult words. "So when you see the desolating sacrilege spoken of by the prophet Daniel standing in the holy place (let the reader understand)" (Matt. 24:15). This language is taken from Daniel 11:31 where it refers to the desecration Antiochus Epiphanes committed in the temple in Jerusalem (see above, pp. 58-59). We know from the parallel verse in Luke 21:20 that it refers also to the overthrow of Jerusalem by the Roman armies in 70 A.D. who desecrated the temple by bringing into its precincts the hated pagan standards. Beyond that it refers to the eschatological Antichrist who will arise in the end time, of whom both Antiochus and Rome were foreshadowings. That he "stands in the holy place" means that he demands the worship of men (see below on II Thess. 2).

The appearance of Antichrist will initiate a fearful persecution of the followers of Jesus. "For then there will be great tribulation, such as has not been from the beginning of the world until now, no, and never will be" (Matt. 24:21). This is the source of the phrase "The Great Tribulation." The point to note here is that in character it is nothing new. Jesus has already told his disciples that they are to expect persecution in the world. Indeed, one of the most central demands of Jesus to his disciples is that they be willing to take up his cross. "He who does not take his cross and follow me is not worthy of me" (Matt. 10:38). "If any man would come after me, let him deny himself and take up his cross and follow me" (Matt. 16:24). The meaning of this is plain. "For whoever would save his life will lose it, and whoever loses his life for my

63

sake will find it" (Matt. 16:25). The cross is not primarily a burden (although it is that indeed); it is first of all an instrument of death. Jesus demands of those who follow him that they must lay their lives on the line; they must be ready to suffer as Jesus suffered. They must be willing literally to lose their lives. There exists between the world and Jesus' disciples an implacable enmity.

To be sure, we experience little hostility in America; indeed, in many cities, it is good for one's business and social standing to be a member of a certain church. This fact has lulled many Christians to sleep in the feeling that God could not possibly allow his people to suffer such a devastating persecution. They cherish the doctrine of a "pretribulation rapture," the belief that the church will be taken out of the world in the Rapture before the Great Tribulation begins. The present author has devoted an entire book to this subject (see G. E. Ladd, *The Blessed Hope,* Eerdmans, 1956) in which he argued that the hope of the Christian is "the appearing of the glory of our great God and Savior Jesus Christ" (Titus 2:13), not escape from tribulation. Interacting with this book, Dr. John Walvoord has written, "The fact is that neither post-tribulationism nor pre-tribulationism is an explicit teaching of scripture. The Bible does not in so many words state either" (John Walvoord, *The Rapture Question,* Dunham, 1957, p. 148. This is an exact quotation from my copy of Walvoord's book. This admission was deleted from subsequent printings of the book).

Be this as it may, it is clear that Jesus taught that all his disciples could expect in the world was tribulation and persecution. As a matter of fact, James the brother of John was the first apostle to be martyred (Acts 12:2), and a probably trustworthy tradition has it that Peter was later crucified in Rome by Nero. The only difference between the normal role of the Christian in the world and the time of the Great Tribulation is the intensity of the persecution. There is no difference in the theology of tribulation. Jesus said, "And if those days had not been shortened, no human being would be saved; but for the sake of the elect those days will be shortened" (Matt. 24:22). God will be caring for his own, even in their darkest hour.

This is expressed in a different way in Luke. Describing the character of the age before the return of Christ, he says, "You will be delivered up even by parents and brothers and kinsmen and friends, and some of you will be put to death. . . . But not a hair of your head will perish" (Luke 21:16-18). How can the hairs of my head be saved if my head is taken off? The meaning is obvious: "Do not fear those who kill the body but cannot kill the soul" (Matt. 10:28). It is obvious in the light of eternity that it is not important how many years I live, or when or how my body dies; what is important is the relation of my soul to Jesus Christ. So God will keep his own safe from (spiritual) harm even in a time of fierce persecution and unparalleled martyrdom.

In verses 29-35, Jesus speaks of the coming on the clouds of heaven of the Son of Man which we usually refer to as the Second Coming of Christ. It will be a cosmic event which will shake the very foundation of the created world. The central theology of the coming of the heavenly Son of Man is that men cannot build the Kingdom of God, nor can history produce it. History, down to the very end, will witness the conflict between the Kingdom of God and the world, which will manifest itself in tribulation and persecution. Only a cosmic act of God, breaking into history from outside of history, can establish his Kingdom.

Then "he will send out his angels with a loud trumpet call and they will gather his elect from the four winds, from one end of heaven to the other" (Matt. 24:31). This is what is generally called the "Rapture" of the church. Paul puts it in somewhat different words, but has the same thought. Immediately after the resurrection of the dead saints, which Matthew does not mention, "then we who are alive, who are left, shall be caught up [raptured] together with them [the resurrected] in the clouds to meet the Lord in the air" (I Thess. 4:17). In fact, the same root word is used in Matthew 24:31, "they will gather," as is used in II Thessalonians 2:1, "our assembling" or "gathering" to meet him.

The important thing to note here is that the only coming of Christ that is spoken of in Matthew 24 is the coming of the glorious Son of Man *after the tribulation* and the only thing that resembles the Rapture is the gathering of the elect from the four winds. There is not a hint of the idea of a pretribulation return of Christ and Rapture of the church before the Great Tribulation. Both of these events clearly happen after the Tribulation. Pretribulationists who plead for a secret coming of Christ to rapture the church somewhere before the Great Tribulation do so by reading something into the text of Matthew 24. The text is utterly silent about any such event.

The next passage that deals with Antichrist is the very difficult passage in II Thessalonians 2. In I Thessalonians Paul has described the Second Coming of Christ to raise the dead saints and rapture the living saints. He opens the second chapter of II Thessalonians by referring to what he had written in the first letter: "Now concerning the coming of our Lord Jesus Christ and our assembling [or gathering] to meet him" (II Thess. 2:1). Then he goes on to say: "That day will not come, unless the rebellion comes first, and the man of lawlessness is revealed" (II Thess. 2:3). This is as clear as language can make it. The return of the Lord and the Rapture of the church must be preceded by a great revolt against God and the appearance of the man of lawlessness, the Antichrist.

Here, several features are revealed about Antichrist which do not occur in either Daniel or the Gospels. He is the man of "lawlessness"; he opposes all law except his own, both the law of God and of man. We have seen this phenomenon in modern times in the totalitarian state. He will be mightily empowered by Satan and will appear to do signs and wonders. He will be supported by many followers who are called the "rebellion," that is, who are against God. The Authorized Version translates it as "the apostasy," but there is no reason to think it means a great apostasy in the Christian church. He will oppose and exalt himself "against every so-called god or object of worship" (2:4). That is, he not only demands the political support of his followers; he will demand universal religious veneration as well. This is further supported by the statement, "he takes his seat in the temple of God, proclaiming himself to be God" (2:4). The general meaning of these words is clear, even if their precise meaning is difficult. Dispensationalists hold that this refers to the rebuilt Jewish temple in Jerusalem where Antichrist will break his covenant with the Jews and demand their worship. However, the words are not meant to be taken so literally. The Old Testament views heaven as God's throne. "Thus says the Lord, 'Heaven is my throne and the earth is my footstool'" (Isa. 66:1; cf. Mic. 1:2). "But the Lord is in his holy temple. Let all the earth keep silence before him" (Hab. 2:20). In Isaiah 14:13 the idea of claiming the prerogative of the heavenly throne of God is attributed to an unnamed tyrant. "You said in your heart, 'I will ascend to heaven above the stars of God. I will set my throne on high; I will sit on the mount of assembly in the far north; I will ascend above the heights of the clouds, *I will make myself like the Most High*'" (Isa. 14:13-14). Against this background, the language in II Thessalonians may be a metaphorical way to describe how the man of lawlessness tries to usurp the place of God and demand that men worship him instead of the Lord.

The thought in 2:6-7 is very difficult: "And you know what is restraining him now, so that he may be revealed in his time. For the mystery of lawlessness is already at work; only he who now restrains it will do so until he is out of the way." There is some principle which restrains the man of lawlessness, embodied in a person; this principle must be taken out of the way to allow the man of lawlessness to come forth.

Dispensationalists take this to be the Holy Spirit who will be taken out of the world when the church is raptured before Antichrist appears. However, since Dispensationalists hold that the Tribulation period will be a time of the salvation of many Gentiles, it is difficult to believe that this refers to the Holy Spirit.

The classical interpretation, which is quite satisfying, is that the hindering power is the principle of law and order embodied in the Roman Empire with the Emperor at its head. Paul tells us in Romans 13:1-7 that such governments are divinely ordained institutions. The function of government, as God has ordained it, is to reward good conduct and punish evil. As such, a ruler is "God's servant for your good" (Rom. 13:4).

This principle can be illustrated by Paul's own experience. More than once he was delivered from the wrath of the Jewish crowd by the just hand of representatives of Rome. One of the most notable instances was his experience in Corinth. Gallio had just come to Corinth as the Roman Governor of the province, and the Jews seized upon this situation as an opportunity to test Gallio. They dragged Paul before his judgment tribunal and accused Paul of subverting Jews from their religious practices. Before Paul could defend himself, Gallio said, " 'If it were a matter of wrongdoing or vicious crime, I should have reason to bear with you, O Jews; but since it is a matter of questions about words and names and your own law, see to it yourselves; I refuse to be a judge in those things.' And he drove them from the tribunal" (Acts 18:14-16).

When the state functions in this way, it functions as an agency with divine approval. The antithesis of this is seen in II Thessalonians in the principle of lawlessness: the deifying of the state and its rulers so that it is no longer an instrument of law and order but a totalitarian system which defies God and demands the worship of men. Then men are no longer punished for doing evil but for doing good. This is the demonic state. Paul sees a day when the rule of law will collapse, when political order will be swept away and be unable any longer to restrain the principle of lawlessness. Then the last defenses that the creator has erected against the powers of chaos will break down completely. This can be understood in the principle of the deification of the state in defiance of the divine ordinance. The principles of both order and lawlessness can be at work at the same time, even in the same state. These two principles will be in conflict during the course of the age. At the very end, law and order will break down, demonic lawlessness will burst forth, and the church will experience a brief period of terrible evil that will be quickly terminated by the return of Christ.

The same basic picture of Antichrist is found in the Beast of Revelation 13. During Paul's missionary journeys Rome was, as we have seen, a friend to Christians. But under Nero, the situation was radically changed and the Christians experienced a short but fierce persecution. The state, instead of a divine ordinance, had become a demonic state. Revelation 13 has a double fulfillment. As Daniel foresees both the Greek Antiochus and the eschatological Antichrist, as our Lord in the Olivet discourse had in view both the fall of Jerusalem and the eschatological Antichrist, so Revelation 13 depicts first Rome and then beyond Rome the eschatological Antichrist.

As in II Thessalonians, Satan is seen as the power behind the Beast. In fact, the Beast arises from the sea in response to the call of the dragon — Satan (Rev. 12:17). We cannot go into detail about the Beast. We must note, however, that besides being empowered by Satan, his main objective is to demand the worship of men (Rev. 13:4).

In addition to this, the Beast was allowed to make war on the saints and to conquer them (13:7). "And authority was given it over every tribe and people and tongue and nation, and all who dwell on earth will worship it, every one whose name has not been written before the foundation of the world in the book of life of the Lamb that was slain" (13:7-8). Here the issue is clearly set forth. On

69

whose side does a man stand? Does he belong to Christ or to Antichrist? The Beast is given power "to conquer," to kill any who do not worship him.

However, there is another side of the picture. In chapter 15 John sees the martyrs standing beside the sea of glass before the throne of God with harps of God in their hands. These are they "who had conquered the Beast and its image" (Rev. 15:2). The Beast has conquered them in martyrdom, but in that same martyrdom *they had conquered the Beast,* for he had been utterly unable to make them deny Christ. This is their victory: loyalty to Christ in tribulation.

There is still another side of the Great Tribulation which is revealed only in the Revelation. It will be the time of the outpouring of the wrath of God upon the Beast and his worshippers. This is pictured in very symbolic language. Seven trumpets are blown in succession and seven bowls or vials of wrath are emptied out upon men. With each trumpet and each bowl, a different plague is visited upon men.

On the eve of the tribulation, John sees two companies of men. The first is pictured as twelve thousand from each of the twelve tribes of Israel. They are sealed with the seal of God on their foreheads; the worshippers of the Beast were sealed with his seal on their hands (13:16). The hundred and forty-four thousand are sealed *so as to be protected from the wrath of God.* This is expressly stated twice. The plague of the fifth trumpet is poured out "only [upon] those of mankind who have not the seal of God upon their foreheads" (9:4). The second bowl is poured out only "upon the men who bore the mark of the beast and worshipped its image" (16:2).

Who are these 144,000? The first answer which suggests itself is that they are literally Jews and picture the salvation of the Jewish people. However, it is impossible for these to be literally Jews, for the twelve tribes listed are simply not the twelve tribes of Israel. Dan is altogether omitted; and Dan is the first tribe mentioned in the division of the land in Ezekiel 48:1. Furthermore, the tribe of Ephraim is also omitted, but it is included indirectly because Joseph was the father of both Ephraim and Manasseh. This means that in reality the tribe of Manasseh is included twice.

What does John mean when he lists twelve tribes of Israel which are Israel but are not literal Israel? He gives us a hint in 2:9 where he speaks of "those who say that they are Jews and are not, but are a synagogue of Satan." See also 3:9: "Behold . . . those of the synagogue of Satan who say that they are Jews and are not." Here is a clear fact: they were people who called themselves Jews, and were in literal fact really Jews, and yet in the spiritual sense they were not really Jews but constituted a synagogue of Satan. In these verses John clearly distinguishes between literal Jews and spiritual Jews. We may believe that John deliberately listed the 144,000 in an irregular listing of tribes to say that here are those who are true spiritual Jews without being literal Jews: in other words, the church.

We have seen that the 144,000 were sealed that they might be sheltered from the wrath of God. We are reminded of Israel in Egypt. They were in Egypt, but they did not suffer the wrath of God as did the Egyptians. So God's people have been delivered from wrath. But as we have found earlier in this chapter, the true church is not to escape tribulation and persecution. Although they will be martyred, not one will be really lost; God has sealed his people and will keep them safe even in martyrdom. We are reminded again of Luke 21:16-18: "Some of you they will put to death . . . but not a hair of your head will perish." So the 144,000 are the church on the threshold of the Great Tribulation: God's people numbered and preserved. The number 144,000, like other numbers in the Revelation, is a symbolic number, representing completeness.

The second throng pictured the same people, the 144,000, seen from a different point of view. They are the church which from the human perspective is a great innumerable throng from every nation and tongue. Now they are seen as martyrs of the Great Tribulation; they are seen standing before God's throne clothed in white robes, singing a hymn of praise "salvation belongs to our God who sits upon the throne, and to the Lamb." They are furthered identified: "These are they who have come out of the great tribulation; they have washed their robes and made them white in the blood of the Lamb" (7:14). Their martyrdom is the path to eternal blessedness and glory.

VII

THE RESURRECTION AND THE RAPTURE

WE HAVE SEEN IN OUR CHAPTER ON THE INTERMEDIATE STATE that the Israelites had no doctrine of the immortality of the soul or of its salvation. We meet in the Old Testament only a few glimmers of the Hebrews' confidence that their God was the master of death and therefore even death could not break the fellowship that God's people had enjoyed with him while living in the flesh.

There is, however, more to be said. There emerges clearly in the Old Testament the confidence in resurrection. Since bodily existence is essential to man, we find a few references to the hope of bodily resurrection. This first appears in Isaiah, although in somewhat ambiguous words: "He will swallow up death forever, and the Lord God will wipe away tears from all faces, and the reproach of his people he will take away from all the earth; for the Lord has spoken" (Isa. 25:8). Resurrection appears in an unambiguous form in Daniel. "And many of those who sleep in the dust of the earth shall awake, some to everlasting life, and some to shame and everlasting contempt" (Dan. 12:2).

Intertestamental Judaism developed this hope in bodily resurrection, but it is not our purpose to tell this story here. Those who are interested will find it spelled out in my book, *I Believe in the Resurrection of Jesus* (Eerdmans, 1975).

When we come to the New Testament, we find the

hope of some kind of blessed existence after death more clearly spelled out (see chapter 3). However, this is not the goal of salvation, and even the New Testament leaves us with many unanswered questions. Since bodiliness is essential to human existence, salvation means the salvation of the *whole man*. "But our commonwealth [citizenship] is in heaven, and from it we await a Savior, the Lord Jesus Christ, who will change our lowly body to be like his glorious body, by the power which enables him even to subject all things to himself" (Phil. 3:20-21).

In the New Testament, the idea and hope of resurrection centers altogether in the resurrection of Jesus. The gospels record that on three occasions Jesus raised the dead (the daughter of Jairus, the son of the widow of Nain, and Lazarus). However, these were not resurrections but resuscitations: the dead were brought back to *physical*, mortal existence, and presumably, after a normal span of years, succumbed again to death. But not so with the resurrection of Jesus. His resurrection means that he has "abolished death and brought life and immortality to light through the gospel" (II Tim. 1:10).

The gospels tell us that Jesus tried to prepare his disciples for his forthcoming death and subsequent resurrection. After Peter's confession of Jesus' messiahship at Caesarea Philippi "he began to teach them that the Son of man must suffer many things, and be rejected by the elders and the chief priests and the scribes, and be killed, and after three days rise again" (Mark 8:31; cf. 9:31; 10:34, etc.). One may well ask if this is true, why the disciples were so utterly crushed when Jesus was seized, condemned, and crucified. The answer is that the contemporary Jewish idea of the Messiah did not make room for dying. The idea of Messiah derives from Isaiah 11 which includes the promise, "he shall smite the earth with the rod of his mouth, and with the breath of his lips he shall slay the wicked" (Isa. 11:4). "Messiah" means "anointed one," that is, the promised, anointed, conquering Davidic King. His mission would be to slay the wicked, not be slain by them. It is of primary importance to realize that the Jews did not interpret the picture of the Suffering Servant of Isaiah 53 as the Messiah. The fact is that this chapter nowhere calls the Suffering One the Messiah. The Jewish idea of Messiah appears clearly in the Gospel of John. After the miracle of the feeding of the five thousand, the people thronged around him to "take him by force and make him king" (John 6:15). A man with such marvelous powers could surely lead the Jews in a victorious conquest over the Roman armies.

It is a simple psychological fact that people do not learn lessons until they are ready for them. So Jesus' disciples never understood his death until after the resurrection, for the cross was, and remains, "a stumbling block to the Jews" (I Cor. 1:23). Thus the record in the gospels is psychologically sound.

We must emphasize that Jesus' resurrection was not a resuscitation — that is, a return to physical, mortal life. We have already quoted Paul to the effect that the resurrection of Jesus means the emergence of eternal life and immortality on the plane of history. No one saw Jesus rise from the dead. He appeared to his disciples; they saw him *after* his resurrection. But no one witnessed the actual resurrection, and this is, as we shall see, because the resurrection transcends all normal "historical" experience.

The earliest account of the resurrection appearances is that of the apostle Paul:

> For I delivered to you as of first importance what I also received, that Christ died for our sins in accordance with the scriptures, that he was buried, that he was raised on the third day in accordance with the scriptures, and that he appeared to Cephas, then to the twelve. Then he appeared to more than five hundred brethren at one time, most of whom are still alive, though some have fallen asleep. Then he appeared to James, then to all the apostles. Last of all, as to one untimely born, he appeared also to me. (I Cor. 15:3-8)

Not all of these appearances are described in the gospels,

especially the appearances to James and to the five hundred. We are here interested primarily in the appearance to Paul on the Damascus Road. There are three accounts of this appearance which differ in some details but agree in the central facts (Acts 9:1-9; 22:6-11; 26:12-18). These accounts tell us that Jesus appeared to Paul in a manifestation of brilliance and glory, and out of the light came a voice which identified itself as Jesus. In other words, Jesus appeared to Paul in what theologians call a theophany — an appearance of God. It may be called an objective vision: it was a vision because the main visual element was brilliance or glory; however, it was objective in that it did not occur in Paul's mind, but outside of him. Attempts have been made to explain this vision on the basis of our knowledge of parapsychology, but such attempts are futile. The vision to Paul transcends all scientific explanation.

The point that Paul is making in his account of the resurrection appearances is that *it was the same Jesus who appeared to him who appeared to the other disciples.* We are not required to think that Paul means to say that the form of the appearances was the same, for as we shall see, they were not. Furthermore, when Paul emphasizes the burial of Jesus, he must have in mind the empty tomb; otherwise there would be no point in mentioning that Jesus was buried.

Thus Paul believed in the *bodily* resurrection of Jesus, although his resurrected state was one of glory instead of the weakness of his physical existence.

That Paul's experience involves a theophany or an objective vision agrees with what Paul says about the risen Christ. "The first Adam became a living being; the last Adam became a life-giving spirit" (I Cor. 15:45). "Christ was raised from the dead by the glory of the Father" (Rom. 6:4). He "will change our lowly body to be like his glorious body" (Phil. 3:21).

The appearances recorded in the gospels appear to be of a very different sort. Matthew records that as the women were leaving the tomb after seeing the angel, Jesus met them "and they took hold of his feet and worshiped him" (Matt. 28:9). Luke records that two disciples on the road to Emmaus recognized him in the act of breaking bread (Luke 24:30-31). Luke further records that Jesus told his disciples to handle his body, to be assured that he was not an apparition: "for a spirit has not flesh and bones as you see that I have" (Luke 24:40). John records that the disciples were gathered in an upper room, "the doors being shut, for fear of the Jews" (John 20:19), when Jesus apparently appeared from nowhere and stood in their midst. There follows the famous story of doubting Thomas who was invited to feel Jesus' wounds in his hands and the spear thrust in his side. The record does not say that Thomas did so, but obviously it was possible or Jesus would not have invited it.

The point is that while Paul's experience must be classified as "an objective vision" — the appearance of the *glorified* Christ — the gospels emphasize Jesus' corporeality. One solution which probably most of my readers will hold is that Jesus was glorified at the time of his ascension. This is possible. However, for reasons which we cannot spell out here, it is equally possible that Jesus rose from the grave in his glorified body, that he appeared in this glory to Paul, but that the appearances recorded in the gospels are condescensions to the earth-bound senses of the disciples (see Ladd, *I Believe in the Resurrection of Jesus,* pp. 127f.). We must remember that the disciples, in spite of Jesus' teaching, were not expecting to see him. All their hopes were incarcerated in the tomb with the dead body of Jesus.

We can imagine their situation if some of us attended the funeral of a friend, saw his casket lowered into the ground, only to be confronted by him face to face three days later. I fear most of us would conclude that our deceased friend had a twin brother whom we had never before seen.

The three facts which emerge from the accounts in

the gospels are these: *identity*. This is the main point. The resurrected Jesus was the same Jesus who was crucified and buried. *Continuity*. Jesus was raised in *bodily* form which was capable of making an impact on the physical senses. As we shall see, Paul insists on the bodily nature of the resurrection. *Discontinuity*. While he was raised in bodily form, it was not the same body. It was a transformed body which possessed new powers. One scholar has expressed it: he was at once sufficiently corporeal to show his wounds and sufficiently immaterial to pass through closed doors. Perhaps this is not an accurate statement. If in his resurrection Christ became a "life-giving spirit" (I Cor. 15:45), we may understand that at the time of the resurrection Jesus passed into the invisible spiritual world. The basic underlying assumption of the whole Bible is that such a world exists. "Now faith . . . is the conviction of things not seen" (Heb. 11:1). The Bible assumes that we are surrounded by the invisible world of God. From it, Jesus was able to appear to people in history, either by way of a glorious theophany, or in more corporeal ways. The conclusion is that "this same Jesus" is today with all of his people in the Spirit and could make himself visible in any way and at any place and at any time he might choose. Jesus was raised in bodily form, but he possessed powers which transcended the ordinary world of time and space.

Perhaps it may seem to the reader that we are devoting too much time to an exposition of Jesus' resurrection when our main concern is the eschatological resurrection of the saints at the end of the age. The reason for this can be readily seen when we recognize that the resurrection of Jesus was itself an eschatological event. By this we mean to say that the resurrection of Jesus was not an isolated event in the midst of history; it was itself the beginning of the eschatological resurrection.

This can be established by numerous passages. Jesus is called the "first-born from the dead" (Col. 1:18). This means not only that Jesus was the first to rise from the dead (Acts 26:23), but as such, he stands at the head of a new order of existence — resurrection life.

This fact can also be seen in the experience of the early church. Acts tells us that the Sadducees were "annoyed because they [the disciples of Jesus] were teaching the people and proclaiming in Jesus the resurrection from the dead" (4:2). This at first is puzzling. It is a historical commonplace that of the Jews, the Pharisees believed in the resurrection of the dead, while the Sadducees denied this doctrine (see Acts 23:7-8). However, they lived together and did not quarrel over points of doctrine like the resurrection of the dead. The fact is, there was a wide variety of views in Judaism about the resurrection (see Ladd, *I Believe in the Resurrection of Jesus*). Why then should it trouble the Sadducees that these disciples of Jesus — this new messianic sect — were preaching resurrection?

The answer is found in the fact that the disciples were not preaching a doctrine, a mere *hope* for the future. They were proclaiming an event in the present which *guaranteed* the future. They were preaching *in Jesus* the resurrection from the dead. Now resurrection was no longer merely a future event, a doctrine, a hope; it had happened in their very midst. If their proclamation was true, it provided an unanswerable denial of the Sadducees' doctrine.

The eschatological character of Jesus' resurrection is most clearly seen in Paul's affirmation that his resurrection was "the first fruits of those who have fallen asleep" (I Cor. 15:20). "First fruits" means very little to the American city dweller. However, in ancient Palestine it carried a vivid meaning. The first fruits was the actual beginning of the harvest which was offered in sacrifice to God for granting a new harvest. It was not hope; it was not promise; it was the actual beginning of the harvest, which was immediately followed by the full harvest.

So Jesus' resurrection bears the character of first fruits. Although it was not *immediately* followed by the resurrection of the saints, it still bears the character of an eschatological event. If we may speak inelegantly, God has split off a portion to the eschatological resurrection and planted it in the midst of history.

This means two things. It is the resurrection of Christ that guarantees the resurrection of believers. Resurrection has become more than a hope; it has become an event. Everything depends upon this event. "If Christ has not been raised, then our preaching is in vain and your faith is in vain. We are even found to be misrepresenting God. . . . If Christ has not been raised, your faith is futile and you are still in your sins. Then those who have fallen asleep in Christ have perished" (I Cor. 15:14-18). Here is an astonishing statement. Can one believe in God and still not believe in the resurrection of Jesus? Does not scripture itself say that "whoever would draw near to God must believe that he exists and that he rewards those who seek him" (Heb 11:6)? Why does faith in God depend on belief in the resurrection of Jesus?

The answer is clear. The God of the Bible is not an aloof deity far removed from man; he is the God who has come near to men in a long series of historical visitations. One scholar has described the God of the Old Testament as "The God who comes." The New Testament record is that this self-revelation of God has come to its fullest degree in the incarnation — in his Word spoken to us in his Son. "The Word became flesh and dwelt among us." Jesus came in the name of the Father claiming to be the Lord over disease — he healed all kinds of illness; over Satan — he cast out demons; over nature — he stilled the storm. But if Christ is not risen, *he is not the Lord of death*. Death has the last word, and the entire succession of revelatory events recorded in the Bible is a *sackgasse* — a dead-end street ending in a tomb.

Christ as first fruits of the resurrection means a second thing. It not only assures our resurrection; it tells us that our resurrection will be like his. When he comes in power and glory, he "will change our lowly body to be like his

80

glorious body, by the power which enables him even to subject all things to himself" (Phil. 3:21). This means that "what is mortal may be swallowed up by life" (II Cor. 5:4).

The question remains: what kind of a body will we have in the resurrection? We have seen that in both Paul and the Gospels, while the resurrected mode of Jesus' existence appears in a different light, three elements are essential: bodiliness, continuity, discontinuity.

We are fortunate to have from Paul's pen a rather lengthy discussion of this very problem. In I Corinthians 15 he deals with one of the questions the Corinthians had raised. "How are the dead raised? With what kind of body do they come?" (I Cor. 15:35). Paul rebukes the questioners rather sharply, "Fool" (I Cor. 15:36). It is not entirely clear what the nature of Paul's opponents was. It may have been on either of two fronts, or possibly on both at once. Paul may have been refuting an overly crass emphasis on the *physical* nature of the resurrection. We know from contemporary literature that some Jews held to a very crude idea of the resurrection (see Ladd, *I Believe in the Resurrection of Jesus*, p. 53), and there appears to have been a "Peter" party, i.e., a Jewish faction in Corinth (see 1:12). However, it is more likely that the problem was with the Greeks who were offended by the idea of resurrection. We know that many Greeks believed in the "salvation" of the soul, but this meant escape from the body. They viewed the body not as something actually evil, but as something that interfered with the cultivation of the soul. The wise man is he who disciplines and controls his body in the cultivation of the soul. The idea of personal immortality would have caused no offense to Greeks, but the idea of bodily resurrection was not a truth they could easily accept.

Paul has already argued that the resurrection of believers is completely dependent on the resurrection of Christ (15:3-19). Now he turns to the further question: the nature of the resurrection body. His first answer is

81

that it will be a body that is different from the physical body. He argues this by establishing that there are different kinds of body. The stalk of green grain that sprouts from the ground is very different in appearance from the apparently lifeless seed planted in the ground. But between the two, in spite of the obvious difference, there is clearly some inexplicable continuity. The solution to this is found in the words, "But God gives it a body as he has chosen, and to each kind of seed its own body" (15:38). So there is a physical body and a resurrection body. They are not the same kind of body; there is difference — discontinuity. But there is also continuity. No seed — no stalk. No physical body — no resurrection body.

Secondly, simple observation proves that there are different kinds of fleshly bodies — one for men, another for animals, another for birds, another for fish. There are many bodies on earth and there are bodies in the sky — the sun, moon, and the stars. But there is obviously a difference in these heavenly bodies. The glory of the sun and moon is vastly greater than the glory of the stars.

Then Paul gives us the nearest thing to a description of the resurrection body to be found in the corpus of Scripture: "What is sown is perishable, what is raised is imperishable. It is sown in dishonor, it is raised in glory. It is sown in weakness, it is raised in power" (15:42-43). The resurrection body will be imperishable, glorious, powerful. Who ever heard of an imperishable body? Every body known on earth is weak and perishable. The new body will be one suited to the life of the world to come.

Paul sums this up by saying, "It is sown a physical body, it is raised a spiritual body" (15:44). It is impossible to translate literally the Greek words Paul uses; they make no sense in English: "it is sown a *soulish* body." By this Paul means to say it is a body animated by and adapted only to the life of the human soul *(psychē)*. It cannot be a body made of *psychē*. In the same way the resurrection body is a "spiritual" body —

not a body made of spirit, but a body transformed by and adapted to the new world of God's Spirit. In view of these facts, the best translation for the *soulish* body is "physical," that is, a body like our present weak, decaying, doomed-to-death, physical body. Some people think that unless one believes in a "physical" resurrected body, he does not really believe the Bible. The real issue is: is the resurrection a resurrection of the *body*? And here Paul leaves us in no doubt.

But again, there is both continuity and discontinuity. The new body has something in common with the physical body; Paul does not tell us what this is. But the risen, glorified Christ met Paul on the Damascus road, spoke to him, and enabled Paul to recognize that it really was Jesus, now risen from the dead.

The important thing is that the resurrection body will be like Jesus' resurrection body. "The first man was from the earth, a man of dust; the second man is from heaven" (15:47). It is not altogether clear what Paul means by the last phrase, whether he is referring to the incarnation, or the resurrection, or the Second Coming of Christ. In the present context it seems best to understand Paul to be referring to the resurrection. In his resurrection and exaltation he returned to heaven — the invisible realm of God's existence — and from this heavenly realm he appeared to the disciples during the forty days, and later to Paul on the Damascus Road. In our earthly bodies we, like Adam, are men of dust — weak, perishable. In the resurrection we shall "bear the image of the man from heaven" (15:49).

It is clear from other Scriptures that the resurrection of the saints occurs at the parousia (Second Coming) of Christ. Paul makes this clear in I Thessalonians: "For the Lord himself will descend from heaven with a cry of command, with the archangel's call, and with the sound of the trumpet of God, and the dead in Christ will rise first" (I Thess. 4:16). That the dead rise "first" is not said with reference to the rest of the dead. The fact is, Paul nowhere in his letters mentions the resurrection of non-saints. "First" means that the dead saints are raised before the living saints are caught up to be with the Lord.

This is paralleled by the resurrection of the saints and of the martyrs in Revelation 20. Revelation 19:11-16 pictures the second coming of Christ in terms of a conqueror. He is seen riding a white horse — a battle charger — riding to destroy Antichrist and those who had followed him. Thus, *after the second coming of Christ* occurs the first resurrection. Revelation 20:4 designates more than one group of people. John saw first those who had been beheaded for their testimony to Jesus. He saw also those who had not worshipped the beast and its image — apparently believers who had escaped persecution. The dead come to life again and rejoice with Christ a thousand years (20:4). Then after the millennial reign of Christ they continue on into the age to come, still in their renewed bodies, in a renewed heaven and earth.

Another event which occurs simultaneously with the resurrection of the saints is what we call the rapture. Paul says in I Thessalonians that immediately after the resurrection of the dead in Christ, "Then we who are alive, who are left, shall be caught up together with them in the clouds to meet the Lord in the air; and so shall we always be with the Lord" (4:17). The word "rapture" comes from the Latin for "we shall be caught up" — *rapiemur*. The catching up of the living saints to meet the Lord in the air is Paul's way of describing the transformation of the living saints when they put on their spiritual bodies like the dead in resurrection without passing through death.

Paul says the same thing in different words in I Corinthians 15:

> We shall not all sleep [in death], but we shall all [both the dead and living saints] be changed; in a moment, in the twinkling of an eye, at the last trumpet. For the trumpet will sound and the dead will be raised imperishable, and we [the living as well as the dead] shall be

> changed. For this perishable nature must put on the imperishable, and this mortal nature must put on immortality. Then shall come to pass the saying that is written: "Death is swallowed up in victory." (15:51-54)

Resurrection for the dead saints; rapture for the living saints. Thus shall all the saints of all ages enter the life of the age to come.

One problem in the Pauline correspondence is the complete silence on the fate of unbelievers. Paul so closely links the resurrection of saints with the resurrection of Christ that it would be easy to conclude that Paul views the fate of the wicked to be left in the grave.

However, other scriptures are not silent on this point. Acts 24:15 quotes Paul as saying that "there will be a resurrection of both the just and the unjust." The Gospel of John is a further witness to the resurrection of all men. Jesus is quoted as saying, "do not marvel at this; for the hour is coming when all who are in the tombs will hear his voice and come forth, those who have done good, to the resurrection of life, and those who have done evil, to the resurrection of judgment" (5:28-29). We are reminded of Daniel 12:2 where some are raised "to everlasting life" and some "to shame and everlasting contempt." It is impossible to say with any certainty that Daniel and John anticipate two resurrections. The most one can say is that both anticipate resurrection of both the righteous and the unrighteous, the former to blessing, and the latter to judgment and condemnation.

However, Revelation 20 clearly anticipates two resurrections. The first resurrection occurs immediately after the victorious Second Coming of Christ and is followed by the millennium. This is called the "first resurrection" (20:6) and issues in life. After the millennial reign of Christ, John sees a great white throne before which the earth and sky fled away, "and I saw the dead, great and small, standing before the throne" (20:12), "and the sea gave up the dead in it, death and Hades [the grave] gave up the dead in them" (20:13) that they might be judged before the great white throne. John does not so designate it, but we must think of this as the second resurrection. However, Scripture is entirely silent as to the nature of this resurrection or the mode of existence of those raised. This is one of the dark places in Scripture where speculation is no virtue. The one thing that is clear is that the second resurrection is one of judgment which leads to the second death.

VIII
JUDGMENT

IT IS A CLEAR TEACHING OF SCRIPTURE THAT MEN ARE individually responsible for their deeds and must face a day of judgment before a holy and righteous God. "It is appointed for men to die once and after that comes judgment" (Heb. 9:27).

Jesus clearly taught a judgment of all men. It will be more tolerable for the people of Sodom and Gomorrah, of Tyre and Sidon, on the day of judgment than for those who heard the gospel on the lips of Jesus and rejected it (Matt. 10:15; 11:22, 24). The men of Nineveh and the queen of the south will arise at the judgment to condemn the blind generation of Jesus. At the close of the age, the wicked and the righteous are to be separated (Matt. 13:40f., 49f.), and all nations will be gathered before the Son of Man (Matt. 25:32) to be judged.

Paul taught that "every man will receive his commendation from God" when the Lord comes (I Cor. 4:5) and that God judges those that are outside (I Cor. 5:13). The saints will judge the world (I Cor. 6:2), but they are to examine themselves lest they be condemned along with the world (I Cor. 11:32). Paul clearly makes no distinction between the judgment of God and the judgment of Christ, for "we shall all stand before the judgment seat of God" (Rom. 14:10) and "we must all appear before the judgment seat of Christ, so that each one may receive

good or evil, according to what he has done in the body"
(II Cor. 5:10).

One of Paul's most important statements about judgment is found in Romans 2:5-10:

> But by your hard and impenitent heart you are storing
> up wrath for yourself on the day of wrath when God's
> righteous judgment will be revealed. For he will render
> to every man according to his works: to those who by
> patience in well-doing seek for glory and honor and im-
> mortality, he will give eternal life; but for those who
> are factious and do not obey the truth, but obey wicked-
> ness, there will be wrath and fury. There will be tribu-
> lation and distress for every human being who does evil,
> the Jew first and also the Greek, but glory and honor and
> praise for everyone who does good, the Jew first and
> also the Greek.

Read superficially, this serves to contradict Paul's
statement often made that man cannot be justified by his
works (Rom. 3:20; Gal. 2:16; 3:11; 5:4). The solution is
found in what is meant by "works." In the latter case,
Paul means works according to an external code — the
Jewish law — which provided a ground for a sense of
human merit and boasting. This does not mean that all
works are unimportant. Paul clearly says, "For God has
done what the law, weakened by the flesh, could not do;
sending his own Son in the likeness of sinful flesh and for
sin, he condemned sin in the flesh, in *order that the just
requirement of the law might be fulfilled in us*, who walk
not according to the flesh but according to the Spirit"
(Rom. 8:3-4). What the external law could not do was to
change the heart of man, to turn him from sinful pride,
to make him love God with all his being and his neighbor
as himself. This the Spirit has done. Another Pauline
term for the good works of Romans 2:5-11 is "the fruit
of the Spirit." This does not mean that the believer puts
God in his debt and receives the gift of salvation *because
he merits it*. It does mean, however, that man, even
Christian man, remains responsible to God, and there
must be the evidence of good works to demonstrate that

he is indeed seeking "glory and honor and immortality." If I may quote a modern commentator, "The reward of eternal life is promised to those who do not regard their good works as an end in themselves, but see them as works not of human achievement but of hope in God" (C. K. Barrett, *Romans,* 1957, p. 117).

In connection with judgment we must look at the biblical concept of the wrath of God, which is the most vivid term we find which designates the relation of God to sinners. Wrath is primarily an eschatological concept. The day of judgment will be a day of wrath for the lost (Rom. 2:5; I Thess. 1:10). The Lord Jesus is to be "revealed from heaven with his mighty angels in flaming fire inflicting vengeance upon those who do not know God, and upon those who do not obey the gospel of our Lord Jesus. They shall suffer the punishment of eternal destruction and exclusion from the presence of the Lord" (II Thess. 1:7-9). Probably Ephesians 5:6 and Colossians 3:6 refer to the impending wrath in the day of judgment.

However, the wrath is not only eschatological; it characterizes the present relationship between God and man. In the present evil age, outside of Christ, men are children of wrath (Eph. 2:3). The wrath of God is revealed against all ungodliness and wickedness of men (Rom. 1:18).

The New Testament concept of the wrath of God is not to be understood in terms of the anger of pagan deities, whose anger could be turned to benevolence by suitable offerings. God's wrath is the implacable divine hostility to everything that is evil, and it is sheer folly to overlook it or try to explain it away. In the New Testament the wrath of God is not an emotion telling us how God feels; it tells us rather how a holy God reacts toward sin and sinners. Wrath is God's personal reaction against sin. Sin is no trivial matter, and the plight of men is one from which they cannot rescue themselves. Wrath expresses what God is doing and what he will do with sin.

There will be a two-fold issue in the day of judgment: acquittal or condemnation. The usual New Testament word for acquittal is justification. Jesus said, "I tell you, on the day of judgment men will render account for every careless word they utter: for by your words you will be justified, and by your words you will be condemned" (Matt. 12:36-37). "Careless words," words spoken spontaneously when one's guard is down, reveal the true character of a man's heart. In this saying, all men will appear before God's judgment, and the issue will be justification or acquittal, or its opposite — condemnation.

Paul has the same situation in mind when he writes, "Who shall bring any charge against God's elect? It is God who justifies; who is to condemn? Is it Christ Jesus, who died, yea, who was raised from the dead, who is at the right hand of God, who indeed intercedes for us?" (Rom. 8:33-34). Here Paul pictures the Christian as standing before the eschatological judgment seat of God; his sins and iniquities condemn him. But he has an intercessor: God himself in the person of Christ has justified him; no one or no thing can condemn him.

The acquitted are not justified by their own works, but by the justification wrought by Christ on his cross. "For our sake he [God] made him [Christ] to be sin who knew no sin, so that in him we might become the righteousness of God" (II Cor. 5:21). Christ was himself free from all stain of sin; but he bore our sins — he *became* sin for us that we sinners might have the righteousness (acquittal) of God reckoned to us. Here is the glory of the Pauline gospel: the judgment which must be rendered in the day of judgment has already been rendered in history by the sacrificial, atoning death of Jesus Christ. Christ has died on his cross, an innocent victim. But in his death he bore the sins of men, he suffered the punishment and the doom which their sins deserve, so that atonement has been made; and this atonement includes justification by faith. Through faith in the atoning work of Christ the believer is justified — here and now — from all the guilt of his sin. He is acquitted.

The essential question is: what is justification? In

Pauline thought justification is the pronouncement of acquittal by the Law-giver and Judge of the universe. Justification, acquittal, is not a subjective ethical quality. It is an objective *relationship* in which God decreed that the believer stands in a right relationship to the Judge of all men. Relationships are real, objective facts.

This is reflected even in our modern concepts of legal justice. A man is accused of a crime. His case is tried before a court. The verdict is either guilty or acquitted. The basic question is not: is he guilty or innocent? The basic question is: what evidence can be provided on the basis of which a decision may be made? If he is pronounced "acquitted," he goes free, even though he may have actually committed the crime. If he is pronounced "guilty," he is punished, even though in some cases he may not have committed the crime. It matters not how he or anyone *feels* about it. The question is: what is the verdict of the court?

So it is with God. God is the universal Law-giver and Judge, and the question is: what is the decision of the heavenly court? Here is a fact that frustrated the Jews: God acquits the guilty. In Jewish thought the sinner must be condemned, the righteous man acquitted. However, Paul proclaimed that in the death of Christ sinners are acquitted of their guilt before God. The death of Christ proves "that at the present time . . . he himself is righteous and that he justifies him who has faith in Jesus" (Rom. 3:26). The death of Christ is both an act of righteousness and an act of love. As an act of righteousness, God in Christ treated sin as it deserved to be treated. "This was to show God's righteousness, because in his divine forbearance he had passed over former sins" (Rom. 3:25). Before Christ, God had not dealt with sin as it deserved to be treated. He seemed to be blinking at man's sin. But in Christ's death he displayed his *righteousness*. He dealt with sin as it deserved to be dealt with.

Here is mystery. What happened on the cross? I do not know; it extends beyond the bounds of human imagination. But in his death Jesus suffered *my* death; he chose *my* doom. We might even say he went to hell in my stead.

All I need to do to avail myself of Christ's acquittal is to accept it by faith. "God justified him who has faith in Jesus" (Rom. 3:26). This is the theme of the Roman epistle: "He who through faith is righteous shall live" (Rom. 1:17). In other words, the man of faith who trusts in the justifying work of Christ on his cross is *already* justified. A cross has become a seat of judgment. The believer is in one sense of the word already on the heavenward side of the eschatological judgment. This is why Paul can write, "There is therefore now no condemnation for those who are in Christ Jesus" (Rom. 8:1).

However, this does not except the believer from the eschatological judgment. "We shall all stand before the judgment seat of God" (Rom. 14:10). The reason for this is to demonstrate that the justification of the believer in history has been confirmed by the works of love he has performed. In other words, justification is by no means a purely legalistic matter so that the justified man can say, "I have been acquitted, so from henceforth, it does not matter how I live." It matters greatly, for the man who has been justified by faith has also by that same faith been joined together with Christ. "How can we who have died to sin still live in it? . . . We were buried with him by baptism unto death, so that as Christ was raised from the dead by the glory of the Father, we too might walk in newness of life" (Rom. 6:2-4). The eschatological judgment of the believer is not to decide whether he is saved or not; it is to confirm his salvation in terms of good words done in the body — in other words, the fruits of the Spirit.

Another passage which deals with the judgment of Christians is I Corinthians 3:10-17. However, here Paul is not dealing with the everyday Christian life as such, but with the work of Christian leaders. We know that the Corinthian church was divided by party spirit, some claiming to be Paul's disciples, others the disciples of

Peter, others of Apollos, still others disdained human leaders and claimed to be followers of Christ alone (I Cor. 1:12). Now Paul deals with the responsibility of Christian leadership in the church. He grants that all are building on the only possible foundation — Jesus Christ (3:11). However, different kinds of structures can be erected on the proper foundation: some of precious materials — gold, silver, precious stone; others on comparatively worthless materials — wood, hay, stubble. In the day of eschatological judgment, the eschatological fire will test all things (see Matt. 3:12). Some buildings will prove to be permanent; others will prove to be worthless and temporary — they will be consumed. Now Paul says something very significant. Some, who have built on Christ and have built enduring structures, will receive a reward (3:14). This is not the reward of salvation or justification, which is always a gift and never a reward. What these rewards are is a matter of fruitless speculation. On the other hand, some have built *on the foundation of Christ* worthless structures, which will be consumed in the apocalyptic fire. However, since he has built on Christ, "he himself will be saved, but only as through a fire" (3:15). Again, we must note that this passage does not apply directly to the ordinary Christian life, but to Christian leaders. "I planted, Apollos watered, but God gave the increase" (3:6). Therefore this passage does not contradict what has already been written about all Christians appearing before the judgment seat of God. It only adds this fact: there will be a special ground for the judgment of Christian leaders.

Another passage from the gospels reflects a judgment determined on the basis of Christian service. Jesus told a parable about a man going on a journey who summoned three of his servants and distributed to one five talents (a talent was probably worth about $1000), to another two talents, and to another one talent, "to each according to his ability" (Matt 25:15). The five talent man earned five talents more; the two talent man earned two talents more; the one talent man was unwilling to risk anything, so he simply laid aside his talent and saved it.

When the Master returned for an accounting, he said to the five talent man, "Well done, good and faithful servant; you have been faithful over a little, I will set you over much; enter into the joy of your master" (Matt. 25:21). The two talent man received exactly the same reward.

Here is a glorious truth. God measures the Christian's service not alone by what he accomplishes but *by the faithfulness with which he has served*.

To the one talent man who had gained nothing Jesus uttered harsh words: "So take the talent from him and give it to him who has ten talents . . . and cast the worthless servant into the outer darkness; there men will weep and gnash their teeth" (Matt. 25:28-30).

If we interpret this strictly according to the letter, it teaches that the faithless disciple will lose his salvation. However, it was Jesus' teaching method to use radical illustrations (see Matt. 18:34), and the thought may well be that a do-nothing disciple is a contradiction in terms. If a professed disciple completely wastes his life so that he counts for nothing in the mission Jesus has given his own, he in effect denies his profession and proves that it is hollow and empty.

The New Testament has a great deal to say about the final condemnation of the wicked. This idea, however, is obscured in the Authorized Version. There are two Greek words which designate the fate of the wicked at death: *Hades* and *Gehenna*. Unfortunately, the Authorized Version translates both of these with the word "Hell." However, Hades is the equivalent of the Old Testament Sheol and should be translated, as the Revised Standard Version does, as either "death" or "the grave" (see Matt. 11:23; 16:18; Luke 16:23; Acts 2:27, 31; Rev. 1:18; 6:8; 20:13, 14). The RSV correctly reserved the word "hell" for the Greek word *Gehenna*. This word is a transliterated Hebrew word which means *ge hinnom* — the Valley of Hinnom. It was a valley south of Jerusalem where children had been sacrificed in fire to Molech (II Chron. 28:3; 33:6). It became a prophetic symbol for judgment (Jer. 7:31, 32) and later for final punishment. Jesus warned that God has the power to cast both body and soul into hell (Luke 12:5; Matt. 10:28; cf. Matt. 5:29, 30). It is pictured as a place of unquenchable fire (Mark 9:43) or eternal fire (Matt. 18:8). The Revelation pictures the final punishment as a lake of fire and brimstone (Rev. 20:10). Jesus said that the wicked will be sent away into "the eternal fire prepared for the devil and his angels" (Matt. 25:41). This lake of fire will be the fate of the beast, the devil, and all whose names are not written in the book of life (Rev. 20:15). The fact that this language cannot be interpreted in terms of physical fire is shown by the fact that death and Hades are also cast into the lake of fire. This is the second death (Rev. 20:14). Our Lord spoke of final punishment in terms of fire (Matt. 13:42, 50; 25:41) or of darkness (Matt. 8:12; 22:13; 25:30; cf. II Pet. 2:17; Jude 13). While both fire and darkness are picturesque ways of speaking of final punishment, they describe the fearful punishment of banishment from the presence and blessings of God in Christ (Matt. 7:23; 25:41).

Paul describes the final state of those who have not obeyed the gospel of Christ by saying, they "shall suffer the punishment of eternal destruction and exclusion from the presence of the Lord and from the glory of his might" (II Thess. 1:9; see I Thess. 5:3). The rebellious and impenitent store up for themselves wrath in the day of wrath when God's righteous judgment will be revealed (Rom. 2:5, 8; see 5:9; I Thess. 1:10; 5:9). Paul also describes the fate of the unsaved by the concept of perishing. This is both a present condition (I Cor. 1:18; II Cor. 2:15; 4:3) and a future doom (Rom. 2:12; II Thess. 2:10). This eschatological doom is also destruction (Phil. 3:19; Rom. 9:22). A companion idea is that of death. Death, in the full meaning of the term, is the penalty of sin (Rom.

5:12; 6:23). While this death is the death of the body (Rom. 8:38; I Cor. 3:22), the term includes much more. This is shown by the fact that it is the opposite of eternal life (Rom. 6:23; 7:10; 8:6; II Cor. 2:16). It is both a present fact (Rom. 7:10f.; Eph. 2:9) and a future fact (Rom. 1:32; 6:16, 21, 23; 7:5). We are reminded of the "second death" in the lake of fire of Revelation 20:14. The central idea is exclusion from the presence of the Lord in his consummated kingdom (II Thess. 1:9) and the subsequent loss of the blessings of life that come with the enjoyment of his presence. However, the terms Paul uses make it clear that it is the just desert of sin and unbelief; but he nowhere describes what this doom involves.

In the picture of final judgment after the millennium, called the "great white throne" judgment (Rev. 20:4), there is a two-fold standard of judgment. First, the books were opened, "And the dead were judged by what was written in the books, by what they had done" (Rev. 20:12). As Paul had said, men will be judged by their works. In Romans 2, Paul says that different men will be judged by the different standards. "All who have sinned without the law will also perish without the law, and all who have sinned under the law will be judged by the law" (Rom. 2:12). The Gentiles who do not have the law of Moses will be judged by the light God has given them in his creation. "For what can be known about God is plain to them, because God has shown it to them. Ever since the creation of the world his invisible nature, namely, his eternal power and deity, has been clearly perceived in the things that have been made. So they are without excuse" for failing to worship God (Rom. 1:19-20).

Gentiles also have an inner light — the light of conscience:

> When Gentiles who have not the law do by nature what the law requires, they are a law to themselves, even though they do not have the law. They show that what the law requires is written on their hearts, while their conscience also bears witness and their conflicting

> thoughts accuse or perhaps excuse them on that day when, according to my gospel, God judges the secrets of men by Christ Jesus. (Rom. 2:14-16)

This suggests, although it does not make it plain, that there will be degrees of punishment, which will be rendered in terms of the way a man has responded to the light he has.

The final norm, however, will be the gospel of Jesus Christ. "Also another book was opened, which is the book of life . . . . and if anyone's name was not found written in the book of life, he was thrown into the lake of fire" (Rev. 20:12, 15).

The judgment of the wicked is not an end in itself, but only a necessary act in the establishing of God's reign in the world. God has done all things possible to bring men to himself: if they reject his grace, they must face his judgment, for in the end God can brook no opposition to his holy will.

Some interpreters have deduced from certain sayings of Paul that Paul expected a final reconciliation to occur which would mean "a universal home-coming" interpreted in terms of a universal salvation of all creatures, both human and angelic. Such an interpretation can indeed be read into several Pauline sayings if they are lifted out of the Pauline context. In Colossians 1:20 Paul speaks of Christ's reconciling all things to himself, whether on earth or in heaven. In Philippians 2:9-11 Paul says that because Jesus has humbled himself in incarnation and death, "God has highly exalted him and bestowed on him the name which is above every name, that at the name of Jesus every knee should bow, in heaven and on earth and under the earth, and every tongue confess that Jesus Christ is Lord, to the glory of God the Father." However, the universal reconciliation spoken of in such passages means that peace is everywhere restored. The universal confession of the lordship of Jesus is not synonymous with universal salvation. There is a stern element in Paul's eschatology that cannot be avoided. There remain recalcitrant wills that must be subdued and which must finally bow before Christ's rule, even though it be unwillingly, that in the end Christ may turn over his kingdom to the Father, that "God may be everything to every one" (I Cor. 15:28).

There remains one passage of scripture which must be dealt with: our Lord's parable of the sheep and the goats in Matthew 25. The Son of Man will come and all the angels with him, and he will sit upon his glorious throne. Before him will be gathered all the nations of the earth, and he will separate them as a Palestinian shepherd separates the sheep from the goats every evening. To the righteous — the sheep on his right hand — he will say, "Inherit the kingdom prepared for you from the foundation of the world" (25:34). Their blessed fate is that they will go away into *eternal life* (25:46). To the wicked — the goats on his left hand — he will say, "Depart from me, you cursed, into the eternal fire prepared for the devil and his angels" (25:41), and their doom will be to go away into *eternal punishment.*

What makes this dramatic parable difficult is the basis of judgment. The righteous go into eternal life because, "I was hungry and you gave me food. I was thirsty and you gave me drink. I was a stranger and you welcomed me. I was naked and you clothed me. I was sick and you visited me. I was in prison and you came to me" (25:35-36). The righteous answer in surprise that they have never seen Jesus hungry and thirsty, a stranger, or naked, or sick, or in prison, that they might minister to him. The judge replies, "Truly, I say to you, as you did it to one of the least of these my brethren, you did it to me" (25:40). The wicked are equally surprised at their judgment, saying they had never seen Jesus in such a state to minister to him. To them Jesus says the same thing: "As you did not do it to one of the least of these, you did it not to me" (25:45).

This is a crucial passage to Dispensationalists, for they make it a separate judgment from the final judgment of men. In the final judgment God is seated upon a great white throne (Rev. 20:11), whereas in Matthew 25 men are gathered before the throne of the Son of Man. Therefore, Dispensationalists see in this parable a judgment of the nations to decide which of them will be granted admission into Christ's millennial kingdom and which will be excluded. "My brethren" are Jesus' Jewish brethren who will be converted during the Great Tribulation and who will go among the Gentiles proclaiming an imminent coming of Christ's millennial kingdom. The Gentile nations who treat Jesus' Jewish brethren kindly, who receive them and accept their message, will be granted admission into the millennial kingdom, and those who abuse them, reject them and their message, will be excluded from the millennial kingdom.

There are three exegetical questions to be considered here. Is this a different judgment from the judgment of the Great White Throne? Does the reward of inheriting the kingdom mean entering the millennium? Are Jesus' brethren his "kinsmen according to the flesh," that is, the Jews?

It seems clear that this judgment cannot be differentiated from the Great White Throne judgment only because the nations appear before the throne of the Son of Man instead of before the throne of God. We have already seen that these two are regarded as the same. It is obvious from the two sayings, "For we must all appear before the judgment seat of Christ" (II Cor. 5:10) and "For we shall all stand before the judgment seat of God" (Rom. 14:10), that the two judgment seats are interchangeable.

Second, the text itself makes it clear that it is not the millennium into which the blessed enter, nor is exclusion from the millennium the fate of the others. The text itself says: "and they [the wicked] will go away into eternal punishment, but the righteous into eternal life" (25:46). Eternal punishment and eternal life. This text speaks not of admission to or exclusion from a temporal earthly kingdom but of the state of final, everlasting punishment and reward.

Third, there is no exegetical reason to understand the brethren of Jesus as his Jewish brethren. On the contrary, we have exegetical evidence that Jesus considered his disciples to be his spiritual brethren. On one occasion Jesus' mother and brothers were seeking opportunity to speak to Jesus, and he replied, "Who is my mother, and who are my brothers?" And stretching out his hand toward his disciples, he said, "Here are my mother and my brothers. For whoever does the will of my Father in heaven is my brother, and sister, and mother!" (Matt. 12:48-50). By this he meant to say that spiritual relationships transcend natural human relationships.

If then the brethren are Jesus' disciples and the judgment a picture of the final eschatological judgment, how may we interpret the passage? The parable pictures the experience of Jesus' disciples as they were to go about preaching the gospel. Not everyone would receive them. Many of their hearers would reject and maltreat them. We must remind ourselves of the character of the earliest disciples' ministry:

> Go your way; behold, I send you out as lambs in the midst of wolves. Carry no purse, no bag, no sandals; and salute no one on the road. Whatever home you enter, first say, "Peace be to this house!" and if a son of peace is there, your peace shall rest upon him; but if not, it shall return to you. And remain in the same house, eating and drinking what they provide, for the laborer deserves his wages. Whenever you enter a town and they receive you, eat what is set before you; heal the sick in it and say to them, "The kingdom of God has come near to you." But whenever you enter a town and they do not receive you, go into its streets and say, "Even the dust of your town that clings to our feet, we wipe off against you!" (Luke 10:3-11)
>
> Behold, I send you out as sheep in the midst of wolves; so be wise as serpents but innocent as doves. Beware of men; for they will deliver you up to councils, and flog you in their synagogues, and you will be dragged before gov-

ernors and kings for my sake, to bear testimony before them and the Gentiles. (Matt. 10:16-18)

In other words, Jesus' disciples as they went about preaching the good news about the Kingdom of God could expect to be hungry and thirsty and naked and imprisoned. But then Jesus said, "He who receives you receives me, and he who receives me receives him that sent me" (Matt. 10:40). In other words, when men and women who had never seen or heard Jesus in person welcomed his emissaries, gave them food and drink, ministered to them when they were flogged or imprisoned, they were doing it as though to Jesus himself. But when men rejected them, turned a deaf ear to them, excluded them from their towns, or even saw them flogged and imprisoned and offered no aid, they were in reality rejecting Jesus himself.

A final question remains to be asked. If this is the final judgment, what do we do about the millennium? There seems to be no room for it. The author is frank to admit that if we had to follow this passage as our program of prophecy, there would be no room for a millennium. I would have to be an amillennialist.

However, this is not intended to be a program of prophecy. It is a dramatic parable. Jesus knows that he is about to leave his disciples in the world with a commission to take the gospel to all nations. He is in effect saying to them, "I am entrusting the destiny of the Gentiles into your hands. Those who welcome and receive you welcome and receive me, and they will be blessed in the day of judgment. Those who reject and exclude and punish you do so to me, and it will go ill with them in the day of judgment."

There is a very different interpretation of the parable which is espoused by many evangelicals. The brethren of Jesus represent all the poor and hungry and naked and disenfranchised of the world. The blessed who inherit the Kingdom are those who have lived out the life of love which is the essential proof of discipleship to Jesus. Such are indeed saved by their works — but not works of legalistic performance but works (or fruits of the Spirit) which flow from a life devoted to Jesus Christ.

There is no theological objection to this interpretation, for we have seen earlier in the chapter that good works in the Christian are to be the outward and visible confirmation of his faith in Jesus Christ. However, there is no other exegetical support for interpreting Jesus' brethren as all unfortunate people; therefore we prefer the former interpretation.

IX

THE KINGDOM OF GOD

WE HAVE ALREADY HAD OCCASION TO TOUCH UPON THE THEology of the Kingdom of God in the chapter on the Second Coming of Christ. There we found that the fundamental biblical way of looking at God and man is that man was created to inhabit the earth, and God again and again visited man in history either for deliverance or judgment. The mission of Jesus of Nazareth is nothing less than such a divine visitation. However, this visitation was a veiled one; Jesus became incarnate as a mortal man of flesh and blood to bring to men in history the blessings of God's Kingdom. However, his mission and meaning were evident only to men of faith. To many others, he seemed to be beside himself (Mark 3:21). His Second Coming is absolutely necessary to display to all the world the lordship that is his even now. In this chapter we will enlarge upon this theology of the Kingdom of God.

It is clear that the Kingdom of God is the central theme of Jesus' teaching. Matthew makes this unmistakably clear. Matthew summarizes Jesus' early ministry with the words, "He went about all Galilee, teaching in their synagogues and preaching the gospel of the kingdom" (Matt. 4:23). The Sermon on the Mount has as its theme the Kingdom of heaven (Matt. 5:3, 10). The great chapter of parables has to do with the Kingdom of heaven (Matt. 13:11). The chapter on fellowship among Jesus' disciples is actually about fellowship in the Kingdom of heaven (Matt. 18:1-4). The great Olivet discourse has to do with the coming of the Kingdom.

To understand this theme more precisely, we must look at a particular word: *aiōn*. There are two words in the Greek New Testament which are translated by the English word "world": *kosmos* and *aiōn*. This is a bad translation and conceals from the reader a very valuable truth. *Kosmos* means "an ordered whole"; it can be used of the universe as a whole, or mankind as a whole, or of mankind as he is seen in his sinful rebellion against God. *Aiōn*, the root of the English word "aeon," is distinctly a time word and means a piece of time of indeterminate length. Greek has no word meaning "forever"; it uses the simple phrase *eis ton aiōna:* into the age.

The most important place that this word occurs in the gospels is in Mark 10. A rich young man came to Jesus and asked what he must do to inherit eternal life (Mark 10:17). By eternal life he meant life in the eschatological Kingdom of God which all the prophets anticipated. The background of his request is Daniel 12:2 — the only place where the phrase "eternal life" occurs in the Old Testament. "And many of those who sleep in the dust of the earth shall awake, some to *everlasting life,* and some to shame and everlasting contempt" (Dan. 12:2). The young man was asking how he could assure himself of participation in the resurrection and participation in the new world of God's perfect rule. Jesus' answer did not satisfy him, and he turned away. Then Jesus said to his disciples, "How hard it will be for those who have riches to enter the kingdom of God" (Mark 10:23), and Jesus said again, "how hard it is to enter the kingdom of God!" (Mark 10:24).

We should here add a parenthetical note for the sake of clarity. The parallel passage in Matthew has a notable variance of words, "It will be hard for a rich man to enter the kingdom of heaven" (Matt. 19:23). "Again, I tell you, it is easier for a rich man to go through the eye of a needle than for a rich man to enter the kingdom of God" (Matt. 19:24). In the first verse, Matthew has "kingdom of heaven," in the second, "kingdom of God." Is there any difference?

Certainly none can be detected from these two verses. In the first verse where Matthew has Kingdom of heaven, Mark has Kingdom of God. Any difference to be found in these texts must be read into them; it cannot be deduced from them. However, Dispensationalists base a whole theology upon a suggested distinction between these two phrases.

How then do we explain the difference? By a single historical fact. "Heaven" is a natural substitute in Jewish idiom for "God." The Jews were very reverent and had a high regard even for the name of God. To illustrate: When the prodigal son came home, he said, "I have sinned against heaven and before you" (Luke 15:18). Jesus himself expressed this high regard. To the Sanhedrin he said, "Hereafter you will see the Son of man seated at the right hand of Power, and coming on the clouds of heaven" (Matt. 26:64). Matthew is the only gospel to use the phrase "the kingdom of heaven"; he was writing for Jewish readers, and this would suit their taste. However, on four occasions he uses "kingdom of God," so we cannot make an absolute rule of it.

To return to our subject: The rich young ruler asked what he must do to inherit eschatological life. Jesus replies by talking about entering the Kingdom of God or the Kingdom of heaven. It is clear that entrance into eternal life is synonymous with entering the Kingdom of God, and both belong to the eschatological order.

This is made even clearer in Mark 10:29-30, where he says that everyone who has suffered physical loss and suffering "in this time" will find blessings to take their place, "and in the age to come eternal life" (Mark 10:30).

The same theology of the two ages is found in Luke 20:35-36: "The sons of this age marry and are given in marriage; but those who are accounted worthy to attain to that age and to the resurrection from the dead neither marry nor are given in marriage, for they cannot die any more, because they are equal to angels and are sons of God, being sons of the resurrection." This age is a time of mortality and death. Marriage is an essential institution or the race would die out. The Age to Come will be inaugurated by the resurrection from the dead, and those who experience it will be like angels in one respect: they will henceforth be immortal, being sons of the resurrection with everlasting life.

The great chapter of parables makes it clear that another event which will introduce the Age to Come is the final judgment, the harvest when the wheat and the weeds are to be separated from each other at the close of (this) age (Matt. 13:39-40, 49).

There are several other places where the idioms of the two ages are used without any theological content to mean "forever." For instance, Matthew 12:32: "Whoever says a word against the Son of man will be forgiven; but whoever speaks against the Holy Spirit will not be forgiven, either in this age or in the age to come." Paul has the same expression: Christ is "exalted above all rule and authority and dominion and power, and above every name that is named, not only in this age but also in that which is to come" (Eph. 1:21).

There are several other passages which speak of the character of this age. In Matthew 13:22 "the care of the age" is hostile to the word of the Kingdom of God and tries to choke out its growth. In Galatians 1:4 Paul calls it "the present evil age." In II Corinthians 4:4 Paul speaks of Satan as the god of this age. In his sovereign wisdom God has allowed Satan to exercise such power that he may be spoken of as the god of this age — the ultimate object of the worship of ungodly men. Of course, everything that Satan does must be done with the sovereign power and consent of God.

Another evil of this age is death. "Since therefore the children share in flesh and blood, he himself likewise partook of the same nature, that through death he might destroy him that has the power of death, that is, the devil" (Heb. 2:14).

In all of these verses from the New Testament we find the same theology which characterizes the Old Testament prophets. It can be charted very simply:

	This Age	The Age to Come
creation		
	Death	Eternal Life

The Day of
the Lord

All the sweep of redemptive history is divided into two ages separated by the Day of the Lord. The New Testament adds several important features to this diagram: the Day of the Lord will witness the coming of the Son of Man, the resurrection of the dead, and the judgment of men.

This is emphasized by Paul when he speaks of the victorious reign of Christ. Speaking of the resurrection Paul says, "Christ the first fruits, then at his coming those who belong to Christ. Then comes the end, when he delivers the kingdom to God the Father after destroying every rule and every authority and power. For he must reign until he has put all his enemies under his feet. The last enemy to be destroyed is death" (I Cor. 15:23-26). Here we have what amounts to a definition of the Kingdom of God. *The Kingdom of God is the redemptive rule of God in Christ, destroying his enemies and by implication bringing to his people the blessing of his reign.*

This makes several conclusions inescapable. The Kingdom of God is the work of God, not of men; nowhere do we find the idiom, much used in some circles, of building the Kingdom of God. To be sure, they may proclaim the work of the Kingdom (Matt. 24:14; Acts 8:12; 28:31), but the Kingdom is ever and always God's Kingdom, God's rule. Furthermore, it is clear that the Kingdom will not triumph in this age. This age remains evil until evil is purged out of his Kingdom by the Son of Man. Again, this shows why the Second Coming of Christ is essential to a biblical theology: apart from his victorious return, there will be no final victory over sin, Satan, and death. However, God's Kingdom is sure to come; all the promises of God remain unfulfilled apart from Christ's return. Finally this theology of the Kingdom of God makes it clear that God's redemptive purpose is not merely a way of salvation for individual souls; it is a purpose for history. We have already tried to make this clear in the chapter on the Second Coming of Christ. Because God has already intervened in history, history has a purpose and a goal; rather we should say that "redemptive" history has a purpose and a goal: the Kingdom of God.

Before we leave the eschatological aspect of the Kingdom, we must consider briefly a much debated question: how and when will the Kingdom come? By "when" I do not mean "when" as we calculate time, but where is that event to be placed in the stress of redemptive history?

We must recognize frankly that in all the verses cited thus far it would seem that the eschatological Kingdom will be inaugurated by a single complex event, consisting of the Day of the Lord, the coming of the Son of Man, the resurrection of the dead, and the final judgment.

However, in the one book which is entirely devoted to this subject, the Revelation of John, this time scheme is modified. Instead of the victory of Christ occurring in a single great event at his Second Coming, Revelation 20 pictures the victory over Satan as occurring in two stages.

As we have seen in an earlier chapter, the demonic powers of evil which oppose both Christ and his church will in the end of time be embodied in an Antichrist who will have power to inflict martyrdom on the saints but who in turn is overcome by the saints' loyalty to Christ. Revelation 19 pictures the Second Coming of Christ. Emphasis is laid altogether on his ability to overcome and destroy the Antichrist. He is pictured as a warrior riding in battle. The Beast in the Antichrist and the false prophet are thrown alive into a lake of fire that burns with brimstone (Rev. 19:20). Then the Seer turns his attention to the conquest of Christ over the power standing behind the Antichrist — Satan. He is first seized by an angel, bound with a great chain, and cast into a bottomless pit, "that he should deceive the nations no more" (Rev. 20:3). This incarceration lasts a thousand years. At the same time John sees the souls of the martyrs who have fallen victims before the Antichrist. "They came to life again and reigned with Christ a thousand years. The rest of the dead did not come to life again until the thousand years were ended. This is the first resurrection" (Rev. 20:4-5). At the end of the thousand years Satan is released from his prison and finds the hearts of men still sinful and rebellious in spite of the fact that Christ himself has ruled over them for a thousand years. They are destroyed by fire from heaven. Then the second resurrection is pictured. "The rest of the dead" (Rev. 20:5), that is, all who had not participated in the first resurrection, are raised to judgment. They stand before God's throne and are judged according to their works. But not only so: "If any one's name was not found written in the book of life he was thrown into the lake of fire" (Rev. 20:15). At this time Christ's victory is complete. The devil is thrown into a lake of fire when he leads the armies against Christ (Rev. 20:10). Now that judgment has been completed, "Death and Hades [the grave] were thrown into the Lake of Fire. This is the second death, the lake of fire" (Rev. 20:14).

The theology that is built on this passage is called millennialism or chiliasm, for it anticipates a reign of Christ over the earth *in history* for a thousand years before the Age to Come is inaugurated. People who hold this view are called "premillennialists" because they believe that Christ will return before his thousand year reign. This is the most natural interpretation of the passage, and it is the view of the present author. One thing

109

must be granted: this is the only place in Scripture which teaches a thousand year reign of Christ. But this should be no objection to the view. After all, no prophet in the later Old Testament period foresaw the church age. They see the future altogether in terms of the Day of the Lord and Israel's role in it. In other words, prophecy telescopes its view of the future.

The greater problem is the theology of the millennium, and here all that Scripture says is that Satan is bound for the thousand years "that he should deceive the nations no more" (Rev. 20:3) as he had done under Antichrist. The idea seems to be that God has determined that there shall be a thousand year period *in history* before the Age to Come when Christ will extend his rule over the nations; that is, that there will be a period of political, social, and economic righteousness before the end. But even in such a society the hearts of men remain rebellious and respond to the devil when he is released, so that in the final judgment the divine decree of condemnation of the wicked will be vindicated.

Many scholars cannot accept this interpretation and picture "the first resurrection" in a different way. A few scholars look upon the thousand years as equivalent to the victorious mission of the church in the world. It is the business of the church not only to save souls, but also to transform by Christian influence the realm of politics, economics, and social activity. Thus the "millennium" — a golden age — will be achieved by God's work in the world in and through the church. Such scholars hold that in spite of the obvious evils in the world, the world is actually getting better and better, and will continue to do so until the golden age is achieved. This view has been held in times past by many scholars. But it is a minority view today. This view is called postmillennialism because the Second Coming of Christ to inaugurate the Age to Come will occur only after the millennium.

Another view is called amillennialism and is defended by many godly, evangelical Christians. This is the view that there is no literal millennium in the future. It is argued that Revelation 20 must be interpreted in light of other Scriptures which place the inauguration of the Age to Come at the return of Christ. The thousand years must be interpreted spiritually as being equivalent to the church age. This view takes two forms. In one form the passage is a prophecy of the fate of the martyrs who have been slain by the beast. Instead of really dying when they were martyred, in reality they lived on after death, sharing Christ's victory and his reign. Satan can no longer hurt them; he is powerless.

A more popular amillennial interpretation is that the thousand years is synonymous with the church age, and pictures the spiritual reign of Christ in the world in and through his church. The difference between this view and postmillennialism is that the reign of Christ through his church does not transform the secular political order so that it becomes the Kingdom of God.

Now it must be admitted that there is some Scriptural support for such a view. Scripture *does* teach that the saints share Christ's victory and reign. "Even when we were dead through our trespasses, [God] made us alive together with Christ . . . and raised us up with him and made us sit with him in the heavenly places in Christ Jesus" (Eph. 2:5-6). Spiritually, we have been raised from the dead, lifted up to heaven itself where we share Christ's session at the right hand of God. This is what Revelation 20 teaches.

While this author does not share this eschatology, one thing is clear: Christians who hold this view do not do so because of a liberal hermeneutic but because they feel the Word of God demands it. However, there is no compelling reason in this author's view for not interpreting this passage in its most natural way — premillennialism.

Before we leave the millennial question, we should note another form premillennialism has taken, that of Dispensationalism. This is probably the most popular form of premillennialism in America. It holds that the millennium is primarily for the Jews. Israel will be restored to her land, will rebuild the temple, and will reinstitute the Old Testament sacrificial system. At this time all of the Old Testament prophecies about Israel as a nation will be fulfilled *literally*. This is deduced from the conviction that God has two distinct and separate peoples: Israel and the Church, with two different programs and different blessings. God's program for Israel is theocratic and earthly; God's purpose for the church is universal and spiritual.

Although he was brought up in this theology, the present author can no longer accept it. The reader is referred to chapter two of this book where the future of Israel is discussed. Hebrews 8 says clearly that the age of types and shadows — the Old Testament cultic system — has been abolished since the reality pictured in the cult has come in Christ. Romans 11 says clearly that Israel as a people are to be saved, but in the same terms of faith in Christ as the church. Today the church is spiritual Israel, and literal Israel is yet to be regrafted back into the olive tree and be included in the true Israel of God. Therefore, it is impossible to view the millennium as primarily Jewish in character.

After the millennium when the Age to Come has been inaugurated, John sees a new heaven and *a new earth,* unto which the holy city, the new Jerusalem, descends. Here is an important fact: the ultimate scene of the Kingdom of God is earthly. It is a transformed earth to be sure, but it is still an earthly destiny. Scripture everywhere teaches this. Paul says that "the creation itself will be set free from bondage to decay and obtain the glorious liberty of the children of God" (Rom. 8:21). Corresponding to the new creation is the resurrection of the body, discussed in another chapter of this book.

The description of the new redeemed earth is highly symbolic. The heavenly city, the new Jerusalem, is pictured as a gigantic cube in shape; it is fifteen hundred miles long, fifteen hundred miles wide, and fifteen hundred miles high (Rev. 21:16). This is obviously a symbolic measurement; it staggers the imagination. The city is surrounded by a wall which is only some two hundred feet high. Why does the heavenly Jerusalem need a wall at all? A wall of two hundred feet is utterly out of proportion to a city fifteen hundred miles high. The answer is not difficult: all ancient cities had walls and John portrayed heavenly realities in earthly language and idiom. The city has twelve gates, each gate a single pearl, representing the twelve tribes of Israel (Rev. 21:12, 21). The streets of the city are like nothing ever seen on earth: transparent gold (Rev. 21:21).

The reality expressed by this symbolic language is clear. "Behold, the dwelling of God is with men. He will dwell with them, and they shall be his people, and God himself shall be with them" (Rev. 21:3). "They shall see his face" (Rev. 22:4). Does God have a face? Ponder this. Try to understand it. "They shall see his face."

At last God's redemptive purpose is fulfilled. Christ has put all his enemies — Antichrist, Satan, sin, death — under his feet. God has gathered a redeemed people from both the Old Testament (Rev. 21:12) and the New Testament times (Rev. 21:14) together on a redeemed earth in perfected fellowship and service and worship of God.

Thus far, we have dealt with the eschatology of the Kingdom of God. We cannot leave this subject without pointing out and expounding the fact that the Kingdom of God is also a present reality. Jesus said, "But if it is by the Spirit of God that I cast out demons, then the *kingdom of God has come* upon you" (Matt. 12:28). Again he said: "Whoever does not receive the Kingdom of God like a child shall not enter it" (Mark 10:15). What do such verses, and others like them, mean?

Let us return to the doctrine of the two ages: this age and the Age to Come. Thus far, we have dealt with the Kingdom of God as it belongs to the Age to Come. But upon further examination we find that the absolute antithesis between this age and the Age to Come must be

113

radically modified. Christ gave himself for us *that he might deliver us* from this present evil age (Gal. 1:4). We are to be *no longer conformed to this age* but transformed by the renewing of our minds (Rom. 12:2). In other words, while we live in the evil age, a new power has broken into it which delivers men and women from it. Again Hebrews 6:5 speaks of those who have tasted the powers of the Age to Come. Living in the old age of mortality, evil, sin, and death, we can experience the life and power of the new age. What does this mean? How does it come about, and what does it mean for the Kingdom of God?

We have defined the Kingdom of God as God's redemptive rule in Christ, destroying his enemies, and bringing to his people the blessings of his reign. We have seen that at the end of the age Christ will destroy the power of Satan in two stages; he will be bound in the bottomless pit for a thousand years, after which he will be cast into a lake of fire. Has Christ already begun to destroy the power of Satan?

The answer is an unequivocal yes. One of Jesus' most characteristic miracles was the casting out of demons. The Pharisees accused him of doing so by demonic power. Jesus replied that such an idea would be ridiculous, for it would mean that Satan's house was divided against itself in civil strife. Then Jesus said, "But if it is by the Spirit of God that I cast out demons, *then the kingdom of God has come upon you*" (Matt. 12:28). Here is a clear affirmation that the kingly reign of God was present and active by the power of the Holy Spirit in Jesus. This means nothing less than the presence of the reign of God, dynamically active in Jesus' mission. Then Jesus said, "Or how can one enter a strong man's house and plunder his goods, unless he first binds the strong man? Then indeed he may plunder his goods" (Matt. 12:29). Satan must be bound before Jesus can deliver demon-possessed men and women from his bondage. Some scholars equate this binding with that of Revelation 20, but the two are placed in entirely different settings.

Our problem with this verse is that "binding" usually means to put completely out of action, but it is clear from the Scriptures that this is not the case here. One of our foremost European scholars has quaintly put it that Satan is indeed bound but with a long rope. The point is that Jesus has invaded Satan's territory — his house — and has rendered him a defeat: he has bound him so that his power is broken.

The same thing is affirmed in different terms in Luke 10:18. Jesus gave his disciples the same power to exorcise demons, and when they reported their success he said, "I saw Satan fall like lightning from heaven." This does not mean that Satan has changed the place of his habitation; it is a metaphorical way of saying that Satan has been toppled from his place of power. He has been defeated by the power of Christ. This says the same thing as Matthew 12:29.

The whole ministry of Jesus constitutes a victory of the Kingdom of God over Satan. Hebrews 2:14-15 says his death meant the devil's defeat: "Since then the children share in flesh and blood, he [Christ] likewise partook of the same nature, that through death he might destroy him who has the power of death, that is, the devil, and deliver all those who through fear of death were subject to lifelong slavery." The crucial word is "destroy." Again, in our idiom "to destroy" means to reduce to nothing, to annihilate. The Greek word does not mean this; it means to render inoperative or ineffective. By both his life and death Jesus has rendered Satan a defeat so that men and women need be no longer in his bondage.

The Kingdom of God means the reign of God in Christ defeating his enemies. "The last enemy to be destroyed is death" (I Cor. 15:26). We have seen that death will be cast into the lake of fire after the millennium (Rev. 20:14). Has Jesus already done anything about defeating death? The answer again is a clear affirmation. He "abolished death and brought life and immortality to light through the gospel" (II Tim. 1:10). Here is an amazing statement. "He has abolished death." He has won a victory over death; he has conquered death.

What can this mean? Obviously it cannot mean that he has annihilated death. Christians die as well as non-Christians, and neither psychology nor physiology can detect any difference between the dead body of a Christian and a non-Christian. Neither can the morticians who prepare the bodies for burial. But is there a difference between the funeral of a Christian and a non-Christian? Indeed there is. For the one it is a final heart-rending good-bye, with no hope for the future. With the Christian, it is *au revoir* or *auf wiedersehen* until the resurrection. Our bodies may die but Christ has brought life and immortality to light. His resurrection is itself an eschatological event. He is the first fruits of the dead, the beginning of the last day. Theologians call such truths as the presence of the Kingdom of God and the resurrection of Jesus "realized eschatology"; a piece of the events of the last day has been split off and planted in the midst of history. We have said that the Kingdom of God is the redemptive reign of God in Christ. Where does Christ begin his redemptive mediatorial reign? Must he "reign until he has put all his enemies under his feet"?

Many premillennialists limit the beginning of Christ's reign to the millennium. But the Scripture is clear that he is already seated at the right hand of God and reigning as King. "He who conquers, I will grant him to sit with me on my throne, as I myself conquered and sat down with my Father on his throne" (Rev. 3:21). Christ is already enthroned, sharing the kingly reign of God the Father. "When he had made purification for sins, he sat down at the right hand of the majesty on high" (Heb. 1:3). Again, "Sit at my right hand till I make thy enemies a stool for thy feet" (Heb. 1:13). The statements that he shares God's throne or sits at God's right hand affirm the same truth: he has been enthroned as King. There is no difference between the kingship and the lordship of

Christ. Because of his obedience in humiliation, God has highly exalted him and given him a name that is above every name, that at the name of Jesus every knee should bow and every tongue confess *that Jesus Christ is Lord,* to the glory of God the Father (Phil. 2:9-11). The name is not Jesus: this was his human name. The name is *Kyrios* — Lord. The verse of exaltation has the same theology as the statement that he must reign until he has put all his enemies under his feet. The day shall come when every man must confess Jesus' lordship and bow before his throne, some willingly, others not. But he shall reign as Lord. His Kingdom shall come and his will be done on earth as it is in heaven.

The primary confession of the New Testament church was the lordship of Jesus. "If you confess with your lips that Jesus is Lord and believe in your heart that God raised him from the dead, you will be saved" (Rom. 10:9). This means two things: I recognize that God has exalted Jesus to be Lord, and therefore I take him as my Lord.

This is the same theology as that expressed in Mark 10:15: "Whoever does not receive the Kingdom of God like a child shall not enter it." The kingly reign of God is a present reality to which I may bow; it will be manifested in power and glory at the end of the age when all men must bow before him.

This structure of the two-age system charted on page 107 therefore needs to be modified, since the powers of the Age to Come do not remain exclusively in the future but have already come to those who are in Christ. We therefore suggest the following chart:

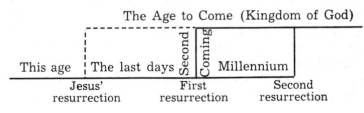

The Age to Come (Kingdom of God)

This age	The last days	Second Coming	Millennium

Jesus'
resurrection

First
resurrection

Second
resurrection

The Kingdom of God belongs to the Age to Come, but as we have seen, the Kingdom of God has already come, not with power and visible glory, but in the meek and humble Jesus of Nazareth. The fullness of the Kingdom of God will not be realized short of the Age to Come. But Satan has already been bound; he has already been defeated and awaits his final doom in the lake of fire.

We have seen that the resurrection — at least of the saints — will take place at the Second Coming of Jesus. However, we have also seen that the resurrection of Christ is nothing but the beginning — the first fruits — of the eschatological resurrection (I Cor. 15:23). Here is another blessing of the Age to Come which has broken into this present evil age. Jesus' resurrection was not the revivification of a corpse; it was the emergence of eternal life and immortality in the midst of mortality (II Tim. 1:10). Thus believers can share Jesus' life here and now while we still dwell in our mortal, dying bodies. This is why John so often speaks of eternal life as a present blessing. This life is knowledge of and fellowship with God the Father through Jesus Christ (John 17:3).

While we share Jesus' life, while we have been raised up from spiritual death to spiritual life (Eph. 2:1-6), our bodies are still mortal and dying. Although the body is dead because of sin, the spirit has been made alive because of righteousness (Rom. 8:10, RSV, NEB). Only in the resurrection at the Second Coming of Christ will believers receive "spiritual bodies" — bodies completely transformed by the power of the Holy Spirit. However, the work of the Holy Spirit is not exclusively eschatological. "Any one who does not have the Spirit of Christ does not belong to him" (Rom. 8:9). God has already given us his Spirit to renew our spirits; in the eschaton, his Spirit will renew our very bodies. This is another foretaste of the blessings of the Age to Come. The present gift of the Spirit "is the guarantee of our inheritance until we acquire possession of it" (Eph. 1:14). The word translated "guarantee" really means "down payment" — much more than a mere guarantee. The Spirit has already renewed us inwardly. This inner renewal is a down payment of the full gift of the Spirit who in the resurrection will renew us outwardly, that is, bodily.

Thus, because of the presence of God's rule in Christ, the Kingdom of God, because of the resurrection of Christ, because of the gift of eternal life, because of the renewal of the Holy Spirit, we live "between the times." We still live in this present evil age. We still have dying, mortal bodies. We are still sinners, even though redeemed. We have entered into a new age, characterized by the overlapping of the old evil age and the Age to Come.

The Bible speaks of this period as "the last days." This is clear from two passages. On the day of Pentecost when God poured out his Spirit, Peter quoted the messianic prophecy of the gift of the Spirit in Joel but added, "And *in the last days* it shall be, God declares, that I will pour out my Spirit upon all flesh" (Acts 2:17). In the Old Testament "the last days" often mean the messianic era, the time of the eschatological Kingdom of God (see Isa. 2:2; Hos. 3:5; Jer. 23:20) at the end of history. Peter places the last days within history. The day of the Lord still lies in the future (Acts 2:20) and is preceded by the last days.

Hebrews does the same thing. God "in these last days has spoken to us by a Son" (Heb. 1:2). Many evangelical Christians think of the last days as the final epoch just before the end. The New Testament equates it with the new era introduced by Jesus and Pentecost. The foretaste of the coming age should make its reality all the more meaningful. The Christian is a man of two worlds; he is destined to inherit the Age to Come because he has already experienced its life and power. This makes the prayer all the more meaningful: "Come quickly, Lord Jesus."